Courtesy of Arizona Photographic Associates,

HUBBELL TRADING POST, established in the late 1870's by Juan Lorenzo Hubbell
his homestead. He called it Ganado, after his friend and sub-chief of all west
Navajos, Ganado Mucho. The Post, still open today, came under the jurisdiction a
administration of the National Park Service in 1967 and is operated by the Sou
western Monuments Association, a nonprofit organization. Trade with the Navajo
carried on in the same manner, but the stock and trade of yesteryear are price
treasures today.

THE
NAVAJO
INDIANS

by Henry F. Dobyns
and Robert C. Euler

Scientific Editors: Henry F. Dobyns and Robert C. Euler
General Editor: John I. Griffin

PUBLISHED BY INDIAN TRIBAL SERIES / PHOENIX

THE NAVAJO INDIANS are the largest single unified native American polity in the United States today. They constitute about one-sixth of the entire Indian population of the country. They are, therefore, the best-known tribe to most citizens, and the single native American group most affecting national Indian policy. How the Navajos reached this pre-eminent position is really an astounding story of adjustment to European culture during historic times.

The prehistory of the Navajos is not nearly so well known to archeologists as is that of the Hopi. It seems fairly certain that they once lived with the great bulk of their linguistic congeners, the Athapascan-speaking tribes of north-central Canada. At some time, probably not much earlier than the first Spanish explorations in the Southwest, the Navajos and Apaches, then one undifferentiated group of hunters and gatherers, moved south along the high Plains hard by the Front Range of the Rocky Mountains. During that migration, they undoubtedly avoided hostile Plains Indians but must have come into some sporadic contact with others. At that time, the Plains Indians were without horses and, especially along the upper Missouri River, led a more sedentary existence than they did in their later heyday. All along the rivers and streams that coursed from the Rockies, Plains Indians were living in palisaded villages and carrying on small-scale agriculture. It was through contacts with native farmers that the migrating southern Athapascans very likely learned the rudiments of farming corn and squash. Later, after the Navajos made contact with the Pueblo peoples of the Southwest, they added to their store of agricultural crops and techniques.

The art of ceramics was another important trait that the ancestors of the Navajos learned from the Plains Indians. Most Navajo pottery is conical with pointed bottoms and flaring rims, almost identical in form to that of the Plains tribes, who, in turn, probably acquired the ceramic art from more easterly Woodland Indians.

The first Athapascans to enter the Southwest, forerunners of later Navajos, were building wooden and stone structures — hogans — in the Gobernador region of northwestern New Mexico

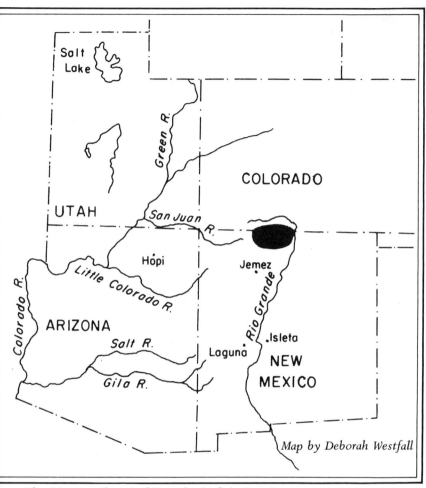

MAP 1. The *Dinexta*, Aboriginal Homeland of the Navajo.

within a century of the time the Spaniards made their initial appearance in the Río Grande region from the south. As early as 1629, Franciscan Friar Alonso de Benavides arranged peaceful relations with Navajos on the Spanish frontier near Santa Clara Pueblo.

Benavides and other Spaniards already distinguished between "Apaches de Navajo" and various Apache bands. To the west of Santa Clara Pueblo in the Gobernador region known to the Navajos as *Dinexta* lay their traditional Southwestern homeland.

The Navajo people speak a southern Athapascan language. In other words, they share the general linguistic pattern of the Apachean peoples known as Jicarillas, Mescaleros, the now extinct Lipans and the Western Apache bands including the Chiricahua, Coyotero and other groups. The differences between the native language of the various Apachean groups and that spoken by the Navajo people is more a matter of difference in dialect than the greater differentiation found between separate and unrelated languages.

Like other southern Athapascans, the Navajo people refer to themselves as the *Nadené*, translatable as "The People." New Mexican Spaniards during historic times modified a Tewa Pueblo term into the word "Navajo" to refer to the *Nadené*.

MAJESTIC ROCK FORMATIONS, eroded from layered sandstone, make Monume

lley beautiful beyond belief.

It is not possible to reconstruct the social and political structure of the Navajo people at the time they first entered the Southwestern region. As a semi-nomadic hunting and gathering people, they probably moved in small, male-dominated extended family groups, each guided by a head man and owing allegiance to no particular other group. The Navajo at that early period were probably bound to each other by no ties other than speaking a common language and sharing a common culture and genetic kinship.

At some period after coming into sustained contact with Southwestern Pueblo societies, probably after the great Pueblo Revolt against the Spaniards in 1680, the Navajo took on at least a veneer of Pueblo social organization. The extended families were further grouped into non-localized matrilineal clans. These clans, made up of both males and females who claimed descent from a known or assumed ancestress, functioned primarily in marriage control. An individual was born into the clan of his or her mother and retained that membership for life. One did not marry a person from the same clan.

Extended Navajo families, though dominated by females as in Pueblo society, exhibited one non-Pueblo feature. They were polygynous. These plural marriages usually took one of two forms. It was preferable for a man to marry two

8

sisters. Because a man moved to the camp of his wife's parents after marriage, this practice of the *sororate,* as it is called, made sense in that it kept maternal relatives together. It was also common for a man to marry a woman and, at the same time, the daughter of that woman by a previous marriage. Thus, a typical Navajo extended family or camp group consisted of maternal grandparents and parents, all their unmarried children, their married daughters and their husbands and offspring.

Several of these extended families usually lived in a particular locality, bounded by visible natural features. These families habitually interacted with one another and so formed an "outfit" or land use community. In historic times such outfits cooperated under two types of leaders, a war leader and a peace leader, each counseling and advising in his particular sphere. There are some vague references to a larger Navajo political grouping, the *natcit,* an annual meeting of headmen. For all practical purposes, however, Navajo political structure did not combine beyond the land use community. There was no "tribe" in the common sense of that term; one *outfit* was in no way responsible for the actions and affairs of another.

RAIDERS

Almost certainly the "Navajo" tag came into Spanish from one of the Pueblo peoples of New

9

Mexico early in the 17th Century when the ancestors of today's Navajo people first came to the notice of European settlers along the Río Grande Valley. Like other southern Athapascans, the Navajos found Spanish settlers a very tempting target for economic raiding. The horses that the Spaniards introduced into the New World constituted a particularly attractive sort of precious good for organized thievery.

There is a lack of direct evidence on the extent to which a mere handful of Navajo ancestors shared in the southern Athapascan territorial expansion undertaken with horses and cavalry weapons and tactics borrowed from the Spaniards. The eastern Apache bands certainly expanded over most of the southern Great Plains during the early 17th Century. Probably the ancestral Navajos shared to some extent in that temporary affluence in terms of horses, saddles, lances, and expanding territory with abundant game.

Southern Athapascan military superiority over other tribes competing for Great Plains hunting territories lasted a century, at most. By 1720, more easterly tribes acquired firearms and munitions from English and French traders that enabled them decisively to defeat the southern Athapascans. Athapascan affluence terminated. In other words, the social and economic benefits of raiding proved somewhat fleeting for the southern Athapascans, who were caught after

1720 between the hammer of the better-armed and also-mounted Plains tribes, and the anvil of the fortified Spanish colonial frontier. Once the Comanches, Pawnees, Wichita and other tribes possessed guns, powder and balls as well as horses, they continuously outfought the Apacheans, who lacked direct access to traders willing to sell them firearms and munitions.

Significantly, the Navajos apparently shared only to a minimal extent in the territorial benefits of the southern Athapascan great century of military expansion. Having ventured farther westward than any other of their southern linguistic relatives prior to the beginning of that expansive century, the ancestral Navajos remained restricted to northern New Mexico with limited access to the big-game riches of the Great Plains. The Jicarillas and other Apacheans more or less cut them off from the rich hunting grounds. On the other hand, once the southern Athapascans were outgunned by other Plains tribes, the Jicarillas and other easterly groups constituted a protective screen between the Navajos and the military giants of the southern Great Plains. Thus, the Navajos suffered less than the other Athapascans from the inroads of the Comanches and other warriors.

Even more important for the long-range course of the Navajo people, Navajo women took up a special economic activity during the expansive century of southern Athapascan history that gave this particular native American group a triadic economy. *They began to raise sheep.*

Just how and where and when the first sheep reached ancestral Navajos cannot be established. The Spaniards introduced sheep, like horses, to the native Americans. Almost certainly the ancestral Navajos first stole sheep to slaughter and eat, before they began raising them. Possibly tender hearted Navajo mothers began to raise sheep by nurturing lambs after the ewes had been slaughtered and eaten. Perhaps captive Navajos assigned to shepherd's tasks by Spaniards walked away home with the flocks. In any event, Navajo women did begin to raise sheep, and the importance of that event in the history of the Navajo people cannot be overemphasized.

When we say that sheep provided the ancestral Navajos with a triadic economy, we contrast Navajo subsistence and nutrition with that of all other native Americans in the early historic Southwest. None of the other southern Athapascans adopted such a rich economic base. They relied upon a dual economy. One component of that dual economy was their aboriginal combination of hunting game that provided animal protein in the diet with wild plant food collecting and gardening that produced some maize, squash and beans. The other economic component was raiding Spanish and sedentary native

12

VAJO GUIDE THEIR FLOCK through mountains of sand in Monument Valley.

American settlements for livestock, food and arms.

The Navajos followed these same economic patterns, but their women added the third component of sheep herding. Economic raiding was essentially a male activity, among native Americans and European settlers alike, just like hunting. Plant food collecting and gardening fell to the women, so that when ancestral Navajo women began tending flocks of sheep, they undoubtedly had to work harder than before and neglect their wild plant food collecting to some extent. That choice paid off astonishingly well.

Navajo sheep flocks provided a far better nutritional base for Navajo life than the earlier always chancy collection of wild plant foods. Domesticated flocks provided animal protein in the Navajo diet on a steady, dependable basis. In the long run, as a matter of fact, Navajo sheep flocks provided more dependable animal protein than the rich big-game resources of the Great Plains gave other southern Athapascans. Even the best of hunters could miss a shot, and even the super-abundant bison of the Great Plains could not always be located when the hunter's family hungered for meat. The sheep that Navajo women herded were, on the other hand, always at hand, always available for slaughtering. Mutton became a principal dietary mainstay for the Navajo people. Navajos began consuming a diet significantly higher in protein than that of other Southwestern Indians.

That nutritional difference made, we believe, a basic difference in the history of the Navajo people. It seems to have affected Navajo fecundity very perceptibly, so that the handful of ancestral Navajos multiplied rapidly throughout historic times, while most other native American populations dwindled.

Conversion of the Navajo household economy to sheep herding evidently had another demographic effect that fostered Navajo population growth. Sheep herding kept Navajo outfits of a few families closely related to each other scattered over a large expanse of territory in pursuit of stock water and good pasturage. For weeks or months at a time, these herding outfits contacted few if any other people. Thus, this type of economic unit minimized the communicability of contagious diseases that decimated sedentary Ameridian populations. While the Hopis (see THE HOPI PEOPLE) and New Mexican Pueblo Indians died by the scores in great smallpox epidemics — in 1780-81, for example — the documentary record gives little or no indication that the Navajo people suffered in any comparable manner.

When Navajo women began raising sheep, they also assured the social leadership of their

15

own sex in herding outfits, nuclear and extended families, and even clans for many decades to come.

Whatever the aboriginal division of labor between the sexes, and whatever the position of Navajo women may have been ancestrally, sheep became women's property and insured women ascendency in social relations. Men might go off to fight and raid, and sometimes return laden with plunder, but women provided the mutton stew day in and day out. Thus, a Navajo woman could divorce her spouse during historic times quite simply. She who controlled the mutton stew pot controlled the household.

Male economic raiding and female property control and inheritance rules are bound to come into conflict, however, and in Navajo life they did so. The male Navajo raiders from time to time brought home war captives. Now no warrior in his right mind would bring back adult male captives to a home camp of twenty to thirty individuals lacking jails, stocks, chains or specialized personnel to put male slaves to work. War captives brought home, therefore, consisted of either young children who could be reared as Navajos, or sexually attractive adult Spanish or Puebloan females.

Navajo men were not so female-dominated that they did not bring home adult female captives they wanted to keep around the house

ANQUILITY for the traditional Navajo psyche.

because of their physical attractions. Such female captives naturally bore children, and thereby created a social and legal dilemma that ancestral Navajos solved with that cultural flexibility that has characterized the Navajo people throughout historic times. Faced with the paradox of female descent-reckoning and offspring of non-Navajo women reared as Navajos, the Navajo people simply recognized that these situations created new Navajo clans. Thus, the Navajo people historically expanded their aboriginal clan system to include a clan for persons descended from Spanish-Mexican mothers, for persons descended from various Puebloan mothers, Ute mothers, and so on.

Navajo men enjoyed the sexual favors of their comely captives, but Navajo women preserved the essential features of female dominance in inheritance and property control by expanding the social system.

At the same time that Navajos have consistently shown themselves to be very adaptable in borrowing such European items as livestock, women and tools, they have retained their own language. This has been and continues to be a tremendous source of social unity among Navajos. While other tribesmen borrowed and more or less modified Spanish or English terms for sheep, horses, slaves, silver, and what not, Navajos usually coined new Navajo terms for new things. For example, they coined the

18

onomatapoetic *"chiddy"* — from the "chuggy-chug" sound of the Model-T Ford — for the automobile. Only infrequently in such instances as terms for "butter" and "money" did they borrow Spanish or English terms. For example, both Navajo *besh* (metal) and *beso* (money) come from the Spanish *peso,* and Navajos write a *chek* just like English speakers.

Religious Change

Most of the Pueblo women who mothered Navajo children joined Navajo society during the decade after the Pueblo Indian revolt of 1680 or after the Spanish Reconquest of 1692. Many of these women joined Navajo society with their husbands and children. Numerous Pueblo refugees chose to move away from their native settlements rather than submit to Spanish rule again after 1692. As described in THE HOPI PEOPLE, hundreds found refuge among the independent Hopi pueblos. Many others chose to settle among the Navajos.

This population increment significantly augmented the Navajo population, as Pueblo refugees became absorbed into Navajo society, learning to speak Navajo, to depend more on sheep flocks than farming, and as women created new Jemez and other Puebloan clans. Quite likely Pueblo refugees established during this period the characteristic Navajo male costume worn for the next two centuries. This consisted of loose white cotton trousers, a loose slip-over blouse or shirt gathered at the waist with a hand-woven sash, and a headband. If reliance on sheep had not already converted Navajo women from wearing tanned skins as their mothers certainly did in aboriginal times, Pueblo refugees persuaded them to wear hand-woven textile dresses and blankets wrapped around the shoulders. Certainly, Navajo women learned the art of loom weaving from their Pueblo neighbors.

Most important of the changes that Pueblo refugees brought to the Navajo people, however, were religious innovations. The aboriginal Navajos apparently devoted relatively little time to religious activity — very likely they were simply too busy hunting and collecting food to stay alive to devote long periods to ritual. Acquisition of the three-pronged economy with sheep as a very dependable source of food enabled the Navajo people to spend more time ordering their relationship with the supernatural. The focus and primary concern of Navajo ritual remained as it surely had been before, curing the sick and avoiding illness.

Navajos believe that it is impossible for them to control nature. Rather, they must live in harmony with it. Persons become ill, in their belief, not because of germs, but because they have fallen out of harmony with the forces of nature. They have dozens of both small and

E MEDICINE MAN AND HIS SAND PAINTING. Each grain of sand and each pattern
s a spiritual meaning in the healing ceremony. These paintings are destroyed
fore sundown the day they are created.

elaborate ceremonies designed to restore that harmony. There is even one important ritual that may be termed preventive medicine; it is geared to preventing people from falling out of harmony with nature in the first place.

Should a Navajo individual fall ill, a diagnostician is first called in. Often this specialist is able to put himself into a trance and, as he examines the patient, his hands tremble over the body. In this way he diagnoses the illness and prescribes the proper ceremony or "sing" designed to cure the patient. Then a "medicine man" or singer is requested to perform the requisite ceremony. Often this singer will construct an elaborate dry painting, another religious behavior borrowed from the Pueblos.

The Pueblo refugees shared the Navajo fundamental concern with well-being. Yet they brought to the refugee camps memories of much more elaborate Puebloan ceremonies, beliefs, and even some diffuse ideas learned from Christian missionaries who resided in various Pueblos for half a century or more prior to the 1680 uprising. Numerous Puebloan beliefs passed into the body of Navajo religious belief as legends, myths and tales were recounted around campfires. Puebloan religious leaders among the refugees evidently consciously trained Navajo singers to some extent in Puebloan rituals and concepts. Many of the major Navajo curing ceremonies feature masked dancers, *yeis*, undoubtedly an imitation of the Pueblo masked *kachinas*. It is clear that the culturally flexible Navajo people gained during this Puebloan refugee period significant religious increments.

SPANISH COLONIAL FRINGE

By the time other Great Plains tribes outgunned the southern Athapascans and sent them reeling west or south into the Spanish colonial frontier, the Navajo people had already achieved their triadic economy and incorporated most of the Puebloan elements they absorbed into their religious system. During the final century of Spanish colonial rule, therefore, the Navajo people lived rather well on the fringe of the frontier of New Spain. Imperial Spanish policy affected the lives of the Navajos differently at various times during that final colonial century.

During that half century after 1720, Spanish colonial fortunes more or less steadily declined on the New Mexican frontier. Plains Indians defeated and massacred a Spanish expedition in 1720, ending for a long time Spanish military power far beyond the established area of settlement. The Navajos understandably took advantage of the relative military weakness of the Spanish colonists. European settlements still constituted attractive targets for Navajo raiders. They contained metal tools, firearms, munitions, foodstuffs and women. Navajo warriors continued to raid Spanish settlements with some frequency. In turn, the Spaniards occasionally managed to locate and attack Navajo outfits, making off with sheep, stored foods, horses, and female captives.

Perhaps more importantly for the Navajo, the colonial Spaniards encouraged their own Indian allies to fight hostile native Americans by purchasing from them children and even older female captives to be baptized and held in household servitude. So important a part of the New Mexican population did such purchased war captives become that a special term, *genízaro,* came to be applied to them. Many Navajo children and women captured and forced into servitude in Spanish households in New Mexico managed to escape and return to their own people. Often such escapees had lived for several months and even years among the Spaniards before they succeeded in evading their masters, so that they learned a great deal about Spanish household and agricultural technology. Thus, they constituted a rather large technological intelligence corps that transfered Spanish techniques to Navajo homes, fields and flocks.

While Navajo warriors carried on economic and retaliatory raiding against Puebloan and Spanish settlements, their wives and daughters continued to tend to the sheep flocks. These continued to grow in numbers, so that this period saw the Navajo people expand their grazing territory appreciably toward the West.

24

Navajo and captive women continued to bear many children, so total Navajo population continued to increase.

Spanish colonial officials regarded Indian warfare as wasteful of resources and unnecessary if only the benighted heathens would see the light of "reason and Christianity." As a matter of fact, the Spaniards had established two missions to the Navajos as early as 1795. While the missionaries failed to convert Navajos, they did attract some of The People whose friendliness toward Spaniards alienated them from other Navajos. Thus, colonial officials from time to time managed to establish contact with Navajo raiding band leaders and obtain peace pacts. Typically the colonial officials mistakenly assumed that each pact would produce instant pacification because they thought that each Navajo leader putting his mark on a treaty was the leader of the entire Navajo population. To be fair to those hard-working colonial officers, the wish was undoubtedly father to the thought. Actually, each Navajo war leader led only a particular raiding band which he was lucky to be able to control inasmuch as success in raiding constituted the principal basis for leadership. Colonial officials were constantly outraged, therefore, when some other raiding band totally ignored the pact reached and attacked a Spanish settlement or allied Indian Pueblo. Spanish-Navajo relations remained in a constant state of

25

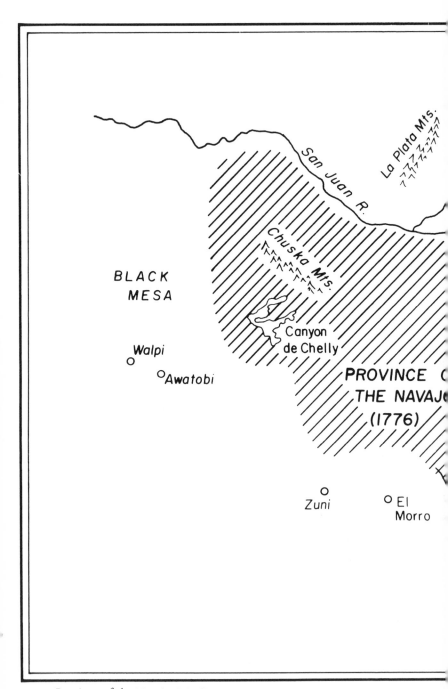

MAP 2 Province of the Navajo (1776).

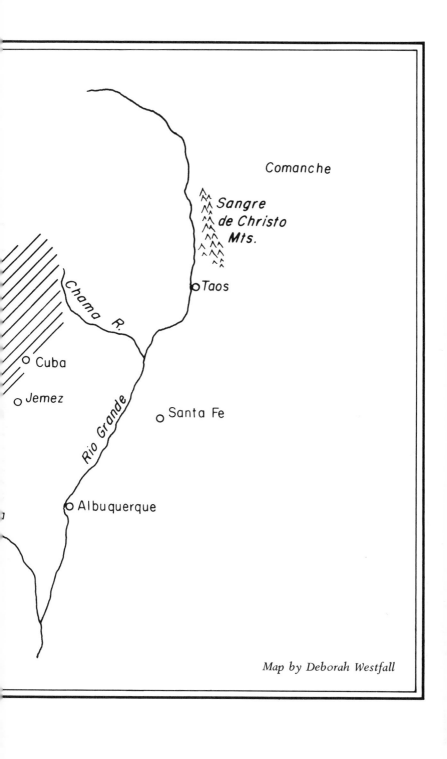

Comanche

Sangre
de Christo
Mts.

Chama R.

○Taos

○ Cuba

○ Jemez

Rio Grande

○ Santa Fe

○ Albuquerque

Map by Deborah Westfall

ferment and distrust, then, for half a century or more.

The quality of leadership provided Spain by its kings changed with the accession of the early Bourbon monarchs, however, and slowly the Bourbon reforms significantly altered the balance of power on the northern frontier of New Spain.

The final half-century of Spanish colonial rule in New Mexico witnessed a drastic change in Indian affairs. Governor Juan Bautista de Anza, a native of Sonora seasoned in the *presidios* of that colonial province, led the Spanish effort that fundamentally altered the position of the Navajo people on the frontier. Anza assumed the provincial governorship during a period when Spain was building its frontier military strength. He could harry the frontier Indians as previous governors had not been able to for many decades. Viceroys and commandants of the Frontier Provinces of New Spain also altered Indian policy in significant ways. Thus, Anza was able to conclude alliances with powerful Plains tribes instead of having to fight them.

With such allies, Anza could bring overwhelming military pressure to bear upon other tribesmen. Thus, he forced the Utes to cooperate with the Spaniards. Using the Comanches and Utes as clubs, he coerced the Navajos into a semialliance with Spain. Anza for the first time split the Navajo people apart from their Apachean relatives. He actually enlisted Navajo auxiliaries for expeditions into Apachean territory, as New Spain gradually pacified the Apaches by constant search-and-destroy missions employing Indian scouts and forces as well as presidial troops. The Navajo people came under Spanish colonial domination, even though colonial authorities did not occupy their land.

MEXICAN RELATIONS

When Napoleon invaded Spain and deposed the King in favor of his brother, Spanish overseas colonies began to disintegrate. Economic resources vanished in the European struggle. Shocked by the easy French conquest, loyal Spanish subjects in the colonies saw their personal interests increasingly diverge from those of residents of the Spanish Peninsula. By 1821, high authorities in New Spain had decided upon political independence, and created the new nation of Mexico.

The turmoil started by Napolean reached the Navajo people in the form of steadily weakening Spanish military power, diminished trade goods, and drastically shaken confidence on the part of colonial officials. Navajos drifted out of the colonial orbit during the closing years of colonial rule. By the time Mexico achieved its political independence, the Navajos lived once

AJOS CAMPED NEAR LAGUNA PUEBLO, NEW MEXICO. Such wagons once formed principle mode of Navajo family transport.

E NAVAJO learned to weave from the Pueblo refugees fleeing the Spanish after the onquest of the 1690's. They became the greatest weavers of the Southwest. ting in front of her hogan, the door of which always faces east, this woman will k for many months in the harsh climate to complete her rug.

again virtually untrammeled by the New Mexican provincial government. Relations between the Navajo people and the Mexicans in New Mexico degenerated into retaliatory raiding. The Navajos raided Mexican settlements and the New Mexicans raided Navajo settlements. The slave trade boomed in New Mexico. Simultaneously, avaricious traders from the United States opened the Santa Fé Trail from Missouri to introduce new cheap merchandise into the Río Grande Valley, whose residents were formerly prohibited from trading with foreigners.

New types of firearms and munitions reached New Mexico to lure Navajo raiders, but also to attract Navajo traders. In this situation, the Pueblo Indians acted as important commercial middlemen. While few Navajos traded directly with New Mexican whites, many traded with Pueblo families.

Whatever their periodic hostilities with various Pueblos, the growing Navajo population included many individuals very interested in Puebloan ceremonials. They attended Pueblo rituals open to outsiders, such as the "Corn Dances" held on Roman Catholic Saint's days. On these occasions, Navajo spectators learned something about the fusion of Roman Catholic and pagan concepts and practices in the various Pueblos. They also carried on a flourishing trade

32

VERSATILITY OF THE NAVAJO WEAVER produces blankets of beauty in design composition, unique in our machine age.

in foodstuffs, metals, arms, munitions, pottery, textiles, and all the products coveted in Navajo hogans.

Laguna Pueblo, founded by Pueblo Revolt refugee descendants who returned from the Hopi country, became a pivotal trading center. Hundreds of Navajos began coming to witness its annual festival, to watch Laguna rituals, and to trade actively for factory and handicraft products and foodstuffs. Thus, the Navajo people entered into a sort of peasant relationship to the commercial economic sector.

As purchasers of manufactured goods passed on through Spanish-speaking traders in Santa Fé or Albuquerque to Puebloan traders, the Navajos possessed significantly more resources than other Southwestern native Americans. Once again, Navajo sheep flocks made the difference. Most Pueblos grazed some sheep, but Apache and Navajo raiders kept their flocks so small that they never became the mainstay of economy or diet as they did among the Navajo people. Thus, Navajo mutton enjoyed brisk demand among the meat-hungry Pueblos.

Moreover, Pueblo weavers had long since shifted their efforts from native cotton to wool as well, so that the wool clipped from Navajo sheep found a ready market in the Pueblos. The Pueblo weavers themselves found that they could easily sell or trade blankets and other textiles to Spanish-Americans or U. S. traders if

34

they did not need them for their own household use.

This steady demand for woolen textiles stimulated Navajo women to develop a significant weaving cottage (or hogan) industry of their own. While they did not adopt the Spanish loom, they either expanded their own aboriginal belt-looms or borrowed and modified the Pueblo man's *kiva* loom for weaving large textiles. Whereas Pueblo men suspended their ceremonial-chamber looms from overhead rafters, Navajo women developed a similar vertical loom supported by thick logs held upright in holes in the earth. While the original Navajo weavers probably worked only to meet family necessities for saddle blankets and dresses, their products quickly found a market at the Pueblo fairs and even in little Mexican stores that acted as concentration points assembling enough local products to sell to Yankee traders or to ship south to Chihuahua.

Very little actual coin entered into transactions at the Pueblo fairs. New Mexico possessed very few coins, so that bartering came to be much more characteristic of local commerce than outright sale for cash. Thus, Navajo-woven blankets, wool and mutton found their own value in haggling transactions. Even captives sold to New Mexicans brought their price in goods rather than coin.

Mexican officials in New Mexico followed the

same pattern as had colonial authorities in negotiating treaties from time to time with Navajo band leaders. Their pacts suffered approximately the same fate of failing to fulfill expectations. Nonetheless, as the New Mexican population expanded, bands of hardy pioneers ventured to settle closer and closer to Navajo grazing lands where streams provided irrigation water. Conflict became inevitable, as two ethnic groups competed for the same resources.

UNITED STATES DOMINATION

The Navajo people lived under nominal Mexican sovereignty for only a quarter century. In 1846, United States troops under the command of General Stephen W. Kearney marched into the province of New Mexico, routed Mexico's forces, and established a military government. United States officials thereby acquired responsibility for the Navajo people as well as numerous other Southwestern Indians. With their scanty sense of or knowledge of history, those officials necessarily learned for themselves the lessons Spanish colonial officials learned decades earlier. Not until U. S. military leaders learned to employ native American scouts and allies against hostile Indians were they to achieve the pacification of the latter.

While the Navajos tended to welcome United States citizens at first, the built-in conflict between Navajo grazers and Mexican irrigation

36

ISELINA" a Navajo maiden photographed by Ben Wittick. Her dress is typical of men's clothing prior to the trading post era of purchasing manufactured cloth.

farmers brought about hostilities between the Navajos and New Mexico's new rulers. Whatever the realities of United States agriculture, U. S. federal officials classically have regarded themselves as representatives of a farming society. Their natural sympathies lay, therefore, with the farmers rather than the pastoral native Americans. The ethnic difference between U. S. citizens and Hispanic farmers in New Mexico also loomed smaller than that between the U. S. citizenry and the native Navajo people.

Military Conquest

United States authorities soon began a series of military expeditions into Navajo country aimed toward militarily defeating the Navajo people and forcing them to accept peace and United States authority on United States terms. This situation continued for fifteen years after the signing of the Treaty of Guadalupe Hidalgo in 1848 that officially transferred New Mexico from Mexican to United States sovereignty.

Like colonial Spain, the United States established a number of military posts on the border of its settled territory in New Mexico and Navajo-controlled lands. Facing at the same time a massive military problem in the hostile Apachean bands, the United States drove a military wedge between the Navajos and the Coyotero Apaches to the south, in order to separate these fighters once again as colonial

38

Governor Anza had decades before (see THE APACHE PEOPLE). The U. S. Army drove directly into Navajo territory to establish one post, Fort Defiance, well within Navajo range.

Despite the efforts of its Indian-fighting army, the United States had not conquered the Navajo people when the social and economic issues of slavery and states' rights precipitated civil conflict in the eastern states. Regular troops garrisoning the posts in and near Navajo territory soon were ordered eastward to the major theaters of conflict. The Navajos appeared to have an open field for raiding operations. Yet, this situation quickly changed as Confederate forces invaded New Mexico from Texas and sought to establish a corridor to California and its rich gold mines and numerous Confederate sympathizers. Union forces marched back into New Mexico, and the large California Volunteer force occupied Arizona and its commander took over the New Mexico territory.

Union authorities raised militia forces in New Mexico, and once that territory had been secured against the Confederate threat, turned again to Indian hostilities.

General James H. Carleton quickly assessed the leadership qualities of the officers available to him for dealing with native American threats to the sedentary population of New Mexico, and recognized that militia Colonel Christopher Carson possessed abilities offered by no other man. He assigned to Carson men, arms and responsibility, and Carson justified that command decision. Carson carried warfare to the Navajo people with an intensity and in a form that they had never before experienced. He swept through Navajo country with militiamen and Indian auxiliaries, seeking and engaging Navajos wherever possible. Carson's men searched for Navajo orchards — The People had planted many peach trees since the Spaniards introduced them into the area — and cut down the trees. They searched for Navajo fields, and burned them or broke the growing plants. They searched for Navajo flocks and herds and killed the sheep and cattle. Carson, in other words, launched an effective search-and-destroy campaign that soon brought Navajos streaming into United States camps and posts to surrender. Carson's columns destroyed the various economic bases of Navajo prosperity, and harried the people so that they dared not even subsist on hunting and food collecting as their ancestors had in the by then remote past.

United States authorities, familiar with that nation's long history of forced relocation of native Americans, moved surrendered Navajos out of their familiar territory to an internment camp. Fort Sumner at Bosque Redondo on the Pecos River at the edge of the Great Plains became the Navajo internment point. Reduced to dependence upon army rations, restricted usually to the camp so they could not hunt or forage for plant foods in the inhospitable environment subject to Plains Indian attacks, the Navajos suffered physical and psychological illnesses. They were a defeated people.

Still, internment camp life with an assured food supply, poor as it was, outraged the Navajo psyche less than the events leading up to it. What really disturbed the Navajo people was the destructive military campaign that laid waste flocks and fields, orchards and horse-herds, food stores and hogans, the total insecurity of life in traditional territory subject to harrassment by U. S. forces. Even worse from the Navajo point of view was the hardship of the journey from the destroyed hogans to Fort Sumner, under armed guard, poorly fed, newly subjected to what seemed to be capricious white authority.

The various unpleasant experiences of the Navajo people came to bear the label "The Long Walk." Like the Cherokee traumas of the earlier "Trail of Tears" from Georgia to Oklahoma, the Navajo traumas of military defeat and internment focused upon the sorrowful trail from homeland to internment more than upon defeat or Fort Sumner itself. "The Long Walk" became a central fact of Navajo psychology for the next century, the foundation stone of Navajo-White relationships, and a fundamental conceptual watershed between the remote and increasingly meaningless past, and the actuality of United

States domination. The United States forcefully pacified the Navajos and their "Long Walk" drove that fact home to them.

Peasant Pastoralism

Once the United States defeated the Confederacy, and the country began trying to mend its internal social and economic scars, federal authorities could cast a glance now and again at the Navajo people. By 1868, federal officials concluded that the interned population at Fort Sumner cost an unnecessary amount of tax money to feed. They also concluded that while the post-war Indian fighting army struggled to defeat the powerful Plains tribes, it was not in the interest of the United States to move the Navajo people into that arena of conflict where they might be tempted to take up arms once again against the Great White Father. Further, federal officials found no great crowd of Anglo-Americans clamoring to occupy former Navajo territory under provisions of the new Homestead Act of 1863. After briefly considering removing the subdued Navajos to Oklahoma, federal authorities decided to allow them to return to a portion of their former haunts upon their promises to remain at peace.

Convinced by their recent traumatic experiences of the futility of further warfare against the United States, the interned Navajo families readily agreed to federal conditions for returning

42

RT DEFIANCE INDIAN AGENCY on Navajo Reservation.

to former territories spelled out in a formal treaty signed on June 1, 1868, at Fort Sumner. The federal government, perhaps conscience-stricken over the destruction of Navajo livelihood or perhaps simply recognizing the economic advantage to taxpayers of making Navajos once again self-sufficient, soon issued returning families small flocks of breeding sheep and goats to enable them quickly to rebuild their pastoral economy. The twelfth article of the treaty provided that the U. S. would appropriate $150,000 to move the Navajos from Bosque Redondo to a new reservation, to purchase 15,000 sheep and goats costing not over $30,000, and to buy 500 beef cattle and 1,000,000 pounds of maize for relief during the winter of 1868-69.

The Navajos agreed to live within a reservation bounded on the north by the 37th parallel north latitude (Arizona's northern border), on the east by a line through Bear Spring (old Fort Lyon), on the south by a line through old Fort Defiance, and on the west by 109° 30 minutes west longitude. They further agreeed to consider allowing other Indians as tribes or individuals to join them in that area in the future. The Navajos relinquished any right to occupy lands outside this reservation, but retained hunting rights on unoccupied lands outside its boundaries. The United States promised to exclude unauthorized persons from that reserved area. It also agreed to construct within it a warehouse, an agency, a carpenter shop, a blacksmithy, a chapel and a school house "so soon as a sufficient number of children can be induced to attend school."

The treaty provided that any family head or single individual over eighteen years of age could select in the presence of the Agent up to 160 acres of land to hold individually instead of communally so long as he and his family cultivated it. Federal treaty-makers clearly had no realistic conception of the semi-arid nature of Navajo territory!

Perceiving formal education as civilizing native Americans, the United States representatives wrote into Article 6 of the 1868 Treaty that Navajos "pledge themselves to compel their children, male and female, between the ages of six and sixteen years, to attend school." That pledge was to be honored more in the breach than in the observance for many decades. Yet when Navajo parents did begin to urge their children to attend school, the federal government would find itself extremely hard-pressed to live up to its obligation stated in the same article: "The United States agrees that, for every thirty children between said ages who can be induced or compelled to attend school, a house shall be provided and a teacher competent to teach the elementary branches of an English education shall be furnished, who will reside among said Indians, and faithfully discharge his or her duties as a teacher."

To further the federal commitment to family farming, the federal representatives included a seventh article in the treaty calling for a $100 subsidy in seeds and agricultural implements to Navajos who selected land and cultivated it. In the following two years, such a Navajo was to receive up to $25 worth of implements and seeds annually. The treaty also provided federal payments to each Navajo of goods that the people could not themselves produce valued at up to $5 on September first of each year for a decade.

Records kept by officials handing out sheep provide a fairly accurate idea of the size of the Navajo population in 1869. While a few Navajos never surrendered and remained at large, most had been interned and sought new breeding flocks. Even after the population losses attendant upon defeat and internment, over 8,000 Navajos were enumerated during sheep issues at Fort Definance, so the total population can be reckoned as possibly 10,000 at that time. The Navajos, even after their defeat and internment, constituted one of the larger tribes in the Southwestern United States, although not comparable in numbers with the Five Civilized tribes at that time.

The Navajo people scattered out over their

NYON DE CHELLY TRADING POST at Chinle, Arizona. S. E. Day, Proprietor.

former territory. They devoted their energies to raising more and more sheep, gardening, and collecting plant foods from a supply that diminished as the wooly flocks consumed the native plants.

At the same time, the people produced a surplus for sale and trade so as to acquire a few items for which they had acquired a taste while interned at Fort Sumner and dependent upon federal rationing. Army rations included that typical United States beverage brewed with hot water and ground-up black tree-seeds, coffee. Navajos adopted coffee as their preferred non-alcoholic beverage. Coffee calls for sugar to sweeten it, and the Navajo people eagerly sought refined sugar, which had not been available to them prior to U. S. sovereignty. The typical sweetener of Mexican and Spanish colonial times was *panocha,* brown lumps used much as white sugar is today.

Army rations relied most of all upon wheat flour, milled to remove the nutritious husks in order to foster rising in making yeast breads. Inasmuch as the Army failed to employ home demonstration agents to instruct Navajo women in baking techniques at Fort Sumner, Navajo women learned to employ white wheat flour to make "fried bread" on a modified Mexican model. Rather than shape the dough into very thin *tortillas,* Navajo woman adopted the quicker course of frying white flour dough in deep fat in skillets.

Coffee, sugar and flour came from overseas or were processed by mills, so Navajo families had to purchase them. Navajo shepherds had, therefore, not only to subsist themselves from their flocks and gardening, but also to produce a surplus for sale. Luckily for the Navajos, their growing flocks of sheep provided that surplus in the form of wool. Navajos could raise sheep for food, slaughter lambs and mature animals for household consumption, tan sheep pelts for hogan use, and still sell the wool they clipped from the remaining animals.

Moreover, the industry of Navajo women processed the wool clip, or a large part of it, into an even more valuable resource, woolen textiles. Washing, carding, dyeing, and then weaving wool into blankets, Navajo women improved their economy by labor intensification of their principal saleable resource. Their textiles found a ready market among Anglo-Americans as saddle blankets, for which they were originally intended, and then as floor throw-rugs, and in the case of the finest artistic products, decorative wall hangings.

The Navajo people did not develop the textile market and wool market on their own initiative. Anglo-American and Mexican-American traders encouraged Navajo production and developed markets for handicraft and raw products. Recognizing that the interned Navajos had acquired a taste for a few commercial items, traders began operating simultaneously with the first issue of sheep to released families. As the Navajo people spread over their former lands again, traders quickly followed them to cater to their appetites for coffee, sugar and white flour. As the Navajo people augmented their flocks, traders accepted wool in exchange for processed foodstuffs, metal tools, saddles and other horsegear, and later wagons and manufactured cloth and clothing.

In different areas at different times, individual traders encouraged Navajo shepherds to raise lambs to market, and shipped them to urban slaughter houses. The lamb market proved to be an undependable and uncertain source of income for Navajo shepherds and traders alike, however, so it never developed into a steady long-term source of income.

The Navajo wool clip, mostly of grades inferior to those produced by English breeds of sheep on eastern farms, sold mostly into the rug manufacturing trade. Innovative traders seeking to expand their own business, encouraged Navajo women to process the best of their wool into hand-woven textiles that could be sold for a higher economic yield that would in turn find its way into the coffers of the traders as Navajos spent their income for manufactured goods and foods. Thus, the Navajo saddle blanket became a

ROADSIDE SHOPPING CENTER near Tuba City offers Navajo beadwork and silver
fts to travelers.

floor rug in Anglo-American homes from coast to coast, with numerous changes in designs and quality.

While the Navajo people lived as peasants in social and geographic isolation from most U. S. citizens, more or less exploited economically by traders, they grew rapidly in population, and by and large enjoyed themselves for several decades. As the people increased in numbers and their flocks expanded, they pressed outward in every direction from their Treaty Reservation. U. S. pacification of once hostile native Americans removed the threat of death and property loss as a deterrant to Navajo territorial expansion. Toward the east, Mexican-American farmers pre-empted springs and flowing river waters for irrigation, limiting the availability of stock water to Navajo shepherds in that direction. Even Anglo-American pioneers moved into the better-watered parts of New Mexico, so the Navajos turned primarily westward.

The Navajo people crept northward into environmental niches once interdicted by hostile Ute Indians. They also advanced northwestward through former Paiute territory (see THE PAIUTE PEOPLE) until they were halted by Mormons spreading southward through Utah. The Navajo people moved southeastward toward Laguna Pueblo and Zuñi Pueblo that had been well within their pre-conquest raiding range.

Finally they halted where the Anglo-American settlers occupied an east-west corridor between them and the White Mountain Apaches.

Toward the west, the Navajos kept going until they crossed the Little Colorado River in significant numbers, entering aboriginal Havasupai territory, advancing almost to the doorsteps of the new Anglo-American settlement of Flagstaff at the foot of the San Francisco Peaks. This westward expansion carried the Navajo people around the Hopi Pueblos, and some of them grazed their flocks closer and closer to those settlements. The expanding Navajo population occupied terrain abandoned by the shrinking Western Pueblo population, leading to enduring and bitter inter-tribal disputes over land use and control on the Hopi mesas.

The peasant pastoral way of life of the Navajo people was sufficiently satisfying to them during the latter quarter of the 19th Century that they did not feel the same psychological pressures perceived by other tribesmen recently defeated by the United States. While other native Americans sought magically to remove the White man from North America by the Ghost Dance movement in 1889 and 1890, the Navajos continued quietly to raise sheep, barter with the traders, and beget more and more children. They ignored the Ghost Dance and continued to graze more land unoccupied by Whites, throwing added pressure on other Indians on all of their borders.

In 1899, the man in charge of the curio department of the Fred Harvey Company took pre-cut Nevada turquoise to a Thoreau, New Mexico, trading post. He persuaded the trader to induce local Navajo silversmiths to make lighter weight jewelry than they had been producing for Navajo customers. The experiment worked, and the company sent raw materials to other trading posts to have made up into jewelry to sell on Santa Fe Railroad trains and stations along its route. Thus, corporate initiative forged yet another link in the economic chains binding Navajos into the national economy. Prior to that time, Navajo silversmiths turned out jewelry and horse trappings for sale or trade to other Navajos, with perhaps not more than one or two smiths alert to the potentials of the Anglo-American market selling silver souvenirs to soldiers stationed at Fort Wingate.

The first Navajo silversmith had learned to work iron before he learned to work silver. He made friends with a New Mexican ironsmith, and learned to make bridles which he traded to other Navajos, and even to Utes for bison hides. He learned smithing early in the 1850's during a period of peaceful relations between his Navajos and Spanish-Americans. The Navajos interned at Fort Sumner still sported many copper and brass

CENTI" AND "GERMANITA" Navajos photographed by Ben Wittick, probably in 1880's. Their clothing, weapons and jewelry reflect a period of cultural nsition from Mexican to Anglo-American influence.

bracelets, but very little silver jewelry, they purchased from Spanish-American silversmiths. Their jewelry was relatively simple in design.

Atsidi Sani, the pioneer Navajo smith, learned to work silver from his Spanish-American mentor after he returned from Fort Sumner. He had already taught his four sons to work iron before the Long Walk. Once he learned to work silver, he trained his sons, and they produced much more silver jewelry than he did. He tended to stick to ironworking. Navajo smiths traded their silver work to Utes just as Atsidi Sani traded iron earlier. Thus, they obtained buckskins, mountain lion pelts, bison hides, skin clothing, and even Ute jewelry fashioned from copper or German silver.

Early Navajo smiths converted many U. S. quarters into silver bells. They scooped a hollow out of a log, and then hammered the quarter down into the cup-shaped hollow with scrap iron rounded on one end. Then they soldered a small loop inside the silver and tied a bit of silver or copper to it for a clapper. Matrons sewed these bells to their sashes so their sons-in-law could hear them moving, and avoid meeting them face-to-face, as Navajo social custom prescribed. Men tied these silver bells to their legs to dance the Yeibichai and war dances.

In the booming Navajo pastoral economy from 1870 to 1900, every Navajo who could afford one purchased a silver headstall for his horse. A silver headstall manufactured from U. S. silver dollars cost a good horse with a saddle and saddle blanket — sixty to $100 at that period.

The Navajo silversmiths fashioned numerous other types of functional objects. Inasmuch as many Navajos still used muzzle-loading guns, the smiths made small powder spoons. As cartridges became available to the Navajos, they abandoned the old muzzle-loaders and most powder spoons were melted to make new things. Other Navajos continued to employ bows and arrows for certain types of hunting, wearing a heavy leather bow-guard to protect their wrists from the snap-back of the bowstring. The silversmiths soon began to fashion cast silver as well as wrought silver decorations for these bowguards, creating one of the most beautiful forms of Navajo silver art, the *ketoh.*

Navajo silversmiths producing for Navajo buyers reached the peak of their artistry making silver tobacco cases. Shaped like small canteens, these were very expensive. Few Navajos could afford them, and Anglo-Americans often mistook them for powder flasks. (Navajos made powder horns from cow horn.) A tobacco case brought a horse or a calf, and few survive today, even in museums.

A more enduring innovation in Navajo silver-smithing occured prior to 1880 with the development of necklaces, first of hollow silver beads, then of what Whites term "squash-blossoms." Actually, the design the Navajos copied from Spanish-American silversmiths in that of a pomegranate blossom, long a feature of Moorish and Spanish horse trappings. Smiths also made *conchas,* or silver disks, to mount on belts, and a variety of buttons.

Around 1880, a Navajo silversmith first mounted a turquoise stone on a silver object. This combination of textures and colors promptly appealed to Navajos, and other silversmiths quickly acquired the necessary tools and techniques. Navajos initially depended upon Santo Domingo and other Pueblo traders to supply their turquoise, but alert White traders quickly perceived the opportunity to profit. Navajo silversmith customers helped to finance the opening of modern turquoise mines in Nevada and Colorado, greatly reducing the price of the stones by 1890. Consequently Navajo smiths also set garnet, jet, malachite or abalone shell in silver during the period when turquoise was costly, but abandoned those alternatives as the price of turquoise fell at the trading posts.

Traders seized other opportunities to profit from Navajo silversmithing. They early introduced manufactured heartshaped bellows to sell, replacing hand-made bellows. Because they make more efficient forges, manufactured buckets replaced hand-made earth or stone forges. Traders stocked crucibles in which to

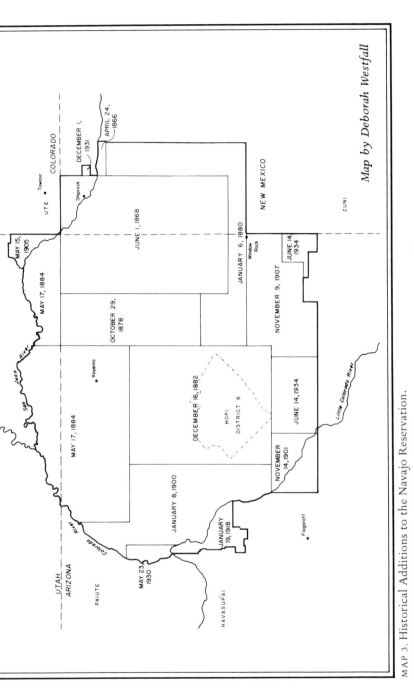

MAP 3. Historical Additions to the Navajo Reservation.

Map by Deborah Westfall

melt silver, sold the smiths pliers, hammers, flat, triangular and rat-tail files, borax to use as flux, sandpaper and emery paper for smoothing. Navajo silversmiths in time learned to file punch designs into scrap iron, and launched into a period of baroque over-decoration with stamped elements.

About 1890, U. S. authorities put Navajo silversmiths even more firmly in the hands of traders than they had been. They began to enforce existing laws against defacing U. S. coins. Traders quickly stepped into the breach and began to import great quantities of Mexican silver *pesos* and other coins. In time, they substituted bar and sheet silver from smelters in the United States. Unable to work U. S. coins they could obtain elsewhere, Navajo silversmiths depended on traders for their raw materials as well as their tools. One enterprising trader even imported Persian turquoise of a bluer shade than the North American stones.

Thus, silversmiths working part-time to make things to sell or trade to Navajo purchasers already fit tightly into the trading post economy by 1889. Then Mr. Herman Schweizer thought of farming out jewelry making through traders to these peasant artisans. Then, by turning out light-weight pieces quickly and without painstaking finishing, smiths expanded their income in cash and kind. Some became full-time jewelry-makers as train passengers proved to be eager customers for Indian handicraft in silver — at a low price.

Silver jewelry attracted great quantities of cash. Other companies emulated the Fred Harvey farming out system, reinforcing trader dominance of smiths. By World War I, some Navajo women took up silversmithing. Factories began stamping out machine-made copies of hand-crafted jewelry.

Perennial Economic Crisis

For half a century, the Navajo people lived the good peasant life as pastoral shepherds integrated into the national economy through scores of trading posts. During that half-century, the Navajo people increased themselves mightily while augmenting their flocks and expanding into new territory, and adopting new clothing and accumulating one precious metal, silver. Federal officials in the Bureau of Indian Affairs slowly built up a bureaucratic apparatus during that half century trying to keep pace with Navajo territorial and population expansion. A series of Presidential executive orders added expanse after expanse of land to the Navajo Treaty Reservation. Beginning in 1878, accessions greatly increased the size of the Navajo territory. Several parcels were added over a span of years starting in 1907. Included was land in

JO CULTURAL distinctiveness and the rugged beauty of the land have endured.

the Four Corners area, and others contiguous to the reservation. Six accessions between 1930 and 1934, plus a later land exchange and a 1962 court decision (Healing vs. Jones) filled out the present reservation boundaries. Finally, however, Navajo expansion reached its limits on all sides. Navajo neighbors, both Indian and White, terminated their outward deployment.

After the turn of the century, the Havasupai people began to recover in numbers and to resist encroachment. The U. S. Forest Service and Anglo-American miners and ranchers blocked Navajo expansion into such of their aboriginal territory as they did not themselves defend. To the north, Paiutes, Utes, and Mormons as well as natural topographic obstacles blocked further Navajo expansion. To the south, White Mountain Apache reserved lands, the Santa Fe Railroad right-of-way and land grant strip as well as Anglo-American ranches and farms closed off further Navajo advance. On the eastern front, Anglo-American and Mexican-American settlers forced Navajo grazers to retreat. Federal land policies created a large "checkerboard" area with alternate sections of land held in federal trusteeship for Navajo use, and alternate sections owned by non-Indians.

Probably the Navajo people began overgrazing their available sheep range soon after the turn of this century, and even earlier in some areas, yet

H CHIS CILLY, maternal great-grandfather of Tribal Chairman Peter MacDonald, a ...itional judge in the late 1800's and early 1900's.

federal officials continued encouraging them to grow more and more sheep. U. S. citizens were not yet conscious of the ecological dangers of over-grazing, and its dire economic consequences. Conditioned by centuries of reliance upon their sheep, the Navajo peasants were themselves in no intellectual position to perceive that their sheep were literally eating themselves out of range.

That the Navajo people could no longer rely on the centuries-old socio-economic adjustment based on sheep herding, even supplemented by weaving and silversmithing began to become painfully apparent when agricultural depression struck the United States following the first World War. The market for Navajo lambs, wool and textiles declined. The Navajo people could still subsist, but by 1920 they had developed all kinds of tastes for processed foodstuffs, and thorough dependence upon manufactured tools and clothing purveyed by scores of trading posts.

Creating a "Tribe"

The U. S. Bureau of Indian Affairs had established prior to 1920 no fewer than six different local agencies to carry out federal responsibilities to the Navajo people. This bureaucracy had implicitly operated rather realistically in terms of the Navajo peasant

NY WHISKERS, a medicine man of the late 1800's and early 1900's and paternal ndfather of Tribal Chairman Peter MacDonald.

economy and segmented socio-political organization. When depression conditions revealed that the entire Navajo population had entered into an enduring situation of economic crisis, responsible officials began seeking a solution. Officialdom tended to think in terms of Navajo-wide programs, and in traditional Anglo-American social structure. That is, officials who had previously treated the Navajo people more or less as the peasants they were, reverted to the Anglo-American concept of "Indian tribe" with chiefs. The fact that the Anglo-American concept of a tribe derived from Germanic models in ancient Europe and seldom if ever fit any native American polity proved no deterrent. United States officials set out to create the Navajo Tribe.

One of the first motives impelling "tribal" organization was discovery that the wastelands the Navajos grazed their flocks over contained underground minerals prized by Anglo-American industrialists. The conditions of federal trusteeship required native American consent to exploitation of such valuable natural resources. Inasmuch as there was no overall Navajo government, one became necessary in the eyes of federal authorities, and to at least some extent in the eyes of formally educated Navajos and wise old men.

In 1921, therefore, federal officials convened

RY CHEE DODGE, distinguished Navajo leader.

a meeting of a "general council" of Navajos at its San Juan Agency to approve leasing land for Anglo-Americans to develop oil and gas wells. That preliminary led to an all-Navajo council set up in 1923, consisting of two delegates from each of the six agencies, with a Chairman. So restricted was this Council that annual meetings dealt in large degree with land leases. Henry Chee Dodge, former interpreter for federal officials in the previous century, served as Chairman of the twelve-man council from 1923 to 1928. His son Thomas Dodge later held that office from 1932 to 1936.

The U. S. Congress passed the Indian Reorganization Act in 1934, encouraging Indian populations to write formal consititutions and govern themselves with elective councils and officers. The Navajo people assembled to discuss the options of that Act and narrowly voted against organizing under its provisions.

U. S. Commissioner of Indian Affairs John Collier provided most of the philosophy behind the Indian Reorganization Act. A long-time defender of native American rights, Collier assumed leadership of the Bureau under President Franklin D. Roosevelt. Despite his almost mystical belief in native American values, Collier also held to environmental conservationist views. When scientists in the emerging U. S. Soil Conservation Service diagnosed the Navajo reservation as very seriously overgrazed, and recommended that the number of animals grazing there be drastically reduced, Collier followed their recommendations.

To the Navajo people "stock reduction" became the second great psychological trauma of U. S. sovereignty, ranking with the Long Walk. Economically dependent upon sheep for centuries, the Navajo peasant pastoralist had developed a very strong psychological dependence upon domestic flocks. He valued livestock above all other possessions. The patter of sheep's hooves in the corral at night lulled him to sleep with the assurance of a full stew pot on the morrow. After a decade of economic depression, Navajo shepherds could envision little or no alternative to subsistence pastoralism when federal minions began slaughtering their sheep. To be sure, Navajo owners received cash recompense for their slaughtered sheep, but cash was soon spent, and animals still missed.

The Bureau of Indian Affairs established a sheep breeding laboratory, and began encouraging Navajo shepherds to add rams to their flocks to up-breed their animals to improve their weight and wool yield, but cross-breeding for improvement took time and patience and an understanding of genetics the illiterate shepherd often did not possess.

Small wonder, therefore, that the Navajo people voted not to organize under the Indian Reorganization Act associated with Commissioner Collier. The only wonder was that the vote was close, and that nativistic reaction was channeled primarily into the peyote church rather than some more extreme sort of movement.

The Bureau of Indian Affairs, with funding assistance through the Civilian Conservation Corps (in which Collier succeeded in having an Indian Division established), launched large-scale range improvement measures, road construction, and other work programs among the Navajos. The federal government greatly expanded its primary school program on the reservation, establishing small schools even in remote regions. Collier made the Navajo people a top priority for Bureau of Indian Affairs economic rehabilitation efforts.

By 1937, the Navajo people were ready to move toward formal governmental organization. A Navajo Constitutional Assembly met to write a constitution. The Secretary of the Interior refused to approve the resulting document, but he did accept regulations that defined election procedures, specifications for a greatly expanded governing council, and other rules. That Constitutional Assembly elected Henry Taliman as Chairman, and he served until the new form of Navajo government began to function after 1938 elections.

The Navajo people elected seventy-four councilmen for the first time in 1938. Jacob

ILDREN OF THE SUN AND SKY – their horizons are the far away dreaminess of sky
d earth bounding their beloved land.

Morgan won the chairmanship for a four-year term.

During the period of the New Deal reformation in Indian affairs, the Bureau of Indian Affairs consolidated its six historic agencies into a single Navajo Agency with headquarters at a new administrative town at a natural rock formation known as Window Rock. A hogan-styled stone building large enough to house the seventy-four member council rose there, and Window Rock began to replace Fort Defiance as the nerve center of Navajo government. Federal officials were well on the way to creating tribal government.

The second World War then significantly affected the Navajo people. First of all, wartime demand restored the market for Navajo wool and other products. Given the limitations on the expansion of the traditional economy, even more important were thousands of wartime jobs that opened up for Navajos. Hundreds of young Navajo men volunteered for "employment" in the U. S. armed services, where they gave a very good account of themselves. They also for the first time in great numbers experienced treatment as social equals by non-Indians.

The United States Marine Corps made imaginative use of Navajos by forming a group of them into radio communications teams. Operating in combat in the Pacific theater of war, these communicators provided field units with an absolutely unbreakable code. The Navajo language was at that time too little known even to scientific linguists for the Japanese to be able to translate Navajo verbal radio messages, much less train soldiers in the field to do so. The Navajo communications men employed code terms for places and things even when speaking Navajo, just to make the task of breaking their "code" even more difficult. Navajos took great pride in these Marine "code-talkers" who held a significant reunion in Window Rock in the summer of 1971.

Thousands of civilian Navajos found factory jobs in southern California and elsewhere, or as unskilled laborers maintaining railroad tracks for wartime heavy traffic, or harvesting wartime crops over much of the Western United States.

Under wartime conditions, the Navajos turned to an elder leader who had long encouraged formal education, integration into U. S. society, and economic enterprise. They elected Henry Chee Dodge Chairman again in 1942, with San Ahkeah as Vice-Chairman. In 1945, Ahkeah ran for the Chairman's job with Chee Dodge the Vice-Chairman candidate. Zhealy Tso served as Vice-Chairman when Chee Dodge died before the end of his term.

While wartime jobs brought prosperity to thousands of the Navajo people, many for the first time, their experiences in field and factory work outside the reservation brought home to them the reality of their handicaps for lack of formal education. Competing with non-Navajos for jobs, pay, housing, and so on, Navajo workers during the war learned how useful were literacy, the ability to speak English and to calculate. Consequently, Navajo adults began to clamor for more educational facilities. Whereas the United States had never had to worry much about fulfilling the educational provisions in Article 6 of the 1868 Navajo Treaty because Navajo parents seldom sent their offspring to school, during and after the second World War the Bureau of Indian Affairs was never able to meet Navajo educational demands. In 1946, there were an estimated 14,000 Navajo children of school age not in school because no schools or teachers were available to them.

Shortly after World War II, the Bureau of Indian Affairs responded to Navajo demands for education in English and related subjects by instituting a special "crash" program. Rather than construct school buildings and recruit teachers to instruct students near their homes, the Bureau obtained a surplus army hospital in Utah and expanded its existing school facilities at Sherman Institute in Riverside, California. There the Bureau transported hundreds of teen-age Navajo youngsters in a massive revival of the boarding school system of native American education that Collier had largely terminated. In special five-year programs, these Navajo teenagers learned, if they achieved the goals set for them by Bureau educational officials, to read and write as well as to speak the English language, some basic mathematical skills and a smattering of vocational skills.

Located in urban areas, these special schools with their massive enrollments also facilitated student learning in such non-academic subjects as beer drinking, pre-marital sexual experimentation, bar-room behavior, cigarette smoking, and gang grouping. Many an adult Navajo with drinking problems today first learned to imbibe while attending one of the special five-year program schools. Many a confirmed fundamentalist Navajo Christian today first succumbed to the temptations of the flesh that led to eventual conversion while attending those same schools. Certainly they rapidly introduced Navajo youths to urban U. S. society.

By the end of World War II, the growth of Navajo population had made it the largest Indian group in the United States. Mass media mention of the Navajo people began to drum this fact of largeness into Anglo-American consciousness — a significant factor in post-war policy making. Awareness of Navajos as the largest native American population in the country contributed significantly to formulating a long-range economic rehabilitation program for the Navajo people at the end of the decade.

The winter of 1947-48 brought very severe

snow storms and ice conditions to the Navajo reservation. By that time, the armed forces veterans had returned home, wartime factory employees had lost their jobs and turned back to the reservation as a refuge. The Navajo people lived in desperate straits, and the blizzards of that winter brought them to the very brink of disaster. In fact, for some Navajos, that winter brought real disaster. Some actually froze to death in the cold or died from starvation. The mass media picked up the grim story of death and disaster, and diffused it throughout the country, calling attention to the plight of native Americans caught in the toils of domestic colonialism just at the time that the nation was launching one of its major post-war economic aid programs overseas.

The crisis of the Navajo people caught the interest and sympathy of the U. S. citizenry in general. Concerned newsmen kept up a drumfire of publicity. Although the U. S. Bureau of Indian Affairs drew a great deal of criticism for conditions it had never been given the financial tools to correct, that organization and the Navajo people benefited in the long run. The Navajo leadership and Bureau officials drew up a Navajo-Hopi long range rehabilitation plan that the U. S. Congress enacted into law. More funds became available for road and school construction, range improvements, vocational on-the-job training, forestry development and industrial development, than ever before. Eighty years after its treaty with the Navajos, the U. S. government moved effectively to integrate the Navajo people into its citizenry, not as illiterate pastoral peasants, but as formally educated wage-earners and entrepreneurs like the rest of its citizens.

Fresh from his leading role as a principal architect of the long-range rehabilitation plan, Chairman Sam Ahkeah won re-election in 1950. That year the Navajo government introduced the use of pictorial paper ballots to replace colored ribbons to identify candidates. The Navajo people were fairly launched on the difficult task of post-war reconstruction of a new economic base to replace the traditional pastoral economy that had served well for centuries, but finally reached a point of no return.

Defense demands for minerals and military research that brought about conversion of uranium ore into nuclear weapons brought the Navajo government high income in this immediate post-war period. The Navajo reservation constituted a major uranium ore resource area. It also provided helium and increasing amounts of natural gas and oil discovered during the wartime scramble to locate such fossil fuels. Corporate enterprise paid the Navajo government well for the privilege of exploiting these newly discovered resources. The Navajo leadership insisted that employment preference be given to Navajos whenever special qualifications did not bar them, thus adding many jobs to the reservation payroll. Fortunately for the Navajo people, a small cadre of Navajo individuals dedicated to the interests of their people had already acquired the formal education and business experience that enabled them to manage the exploding economic empire that emerged rapidly during Ahkeah's second term as Chairman.

The fantastic expansion of tribal income and the skill with which dedicated leaders husbanded it for investment to benefit all Navajos instead of distributing it in what would have been small per capital payments, generated voter dissatisfaction with Ahkeah's leadership.

When a Navajo with experience in urban U. S. business enterprise and society ran against Ahkeah in 1954, he defeated the incumbent Chairman. Paul Jones carried Scott Prescott into office as Vice-Chairman. Jones also brought to the forefront of Navajo tribal politics an overt linkage to the national Republican party. The Navajo electorate had been rather solidly anti-Democratic ever since John Collier pushed stock reduction early in the Roosevelt administration. Not many Navajos possessed the literacy qualifications to vote, and in any event neither New Mexico nor Arizona permitted Indians dwelling on reservations to vote until 1948. Inasmuch as the long-range rehabilitation program was launched under a Democratic national administration, the Navajo leadership then acquired at least some aura of guilt by association. When Dwight D. Eisenhower won the presidency in 1952 and Arizona Republican Barry Goldwater won election to the U. S. Senate, the stage was ready for frankly partisan behavior by Navajo political leaders.

As Navajo Tribal Chairman, Paul Jones capitalized effectively upon his political predilections to continue obtaining federal investment in the creation of a viable wage economy in Navajoland. The eighty-nine million dollar ten-year rehabilitation program by the end of Jones's term had poured thirty-eight million dollars into road construction and twenty-five million into building schools. Persuading Congress to appropriate educational funds over and above the rehabilitation program levels, Jones and other leaders saw the percentage of Navajo school-age children in school rise from 62 percent in 1954 to 93 percent in 1958.

Navajo health problems by the time Jones took office became painfully apparent to federal officials and to medical practitioners called upon to help reservation health authorities meet emergency epidemic crises. Advice from some of these medical experts from institutions such as Cornell University's Medical College, as well as influence from native American leaders such as Jones led the Eisenhower administration to

81

transfer responsibility for Indian health from the Bureau of Indian Affairs to the U. S. Public Health Service in 1955. As a uniformed federal service, the USPHS could draw upon the national pool of medical doctors serving their national service obligation to staff remote hospitals and clinics on the vast Navajo reservation – the most pressing single problem area of the entire Indian health field. Medical researchers trained Navajo health aides and devised other innovations for delivering modern health services to isolated hogans, thus dramatically cutting the tuberculosis infections that had constituted a principal illness. They failed to achieve similar impact on all other ailments, yet they significantly advanced the integration of Navajo medical care with that of the rest of the nation. Thereby, the medical researchers and the practitioners who put into everyday use their findings insured a continuation of the rapid rise of Navajo population.

Running a competent administration in the midst of the Eisenhower years, Paul Jones won re-election as Chairman in 1958. That year the national regime backed off from its energetic support of termination of federal services to native Americans, state legal jurisdiction over reservations, and related measures that disturbed many reservation residents. It continued, however, its massive financial commitment to the urban relocation program launched under former President Harry Truman by Commissioner Dillon Myer. The Bureau of Indian Affairs maintained relocation offices in cities such as Chicago, Denver and San Francisco, with personnel there to help native American migrants find jobs, housing, transportation, and to counsel them on economic purchasing and other matters. As the largest single Indian group in the country, the Navajos naturally formed a major clientele for the relocation program. Bureau recruiters energetically encouraged Navajo families to move to the urban centers.

As large corporations exploited reservation resources, and the rehabilitation program investments created new industries and occupations, the wage-work sector of the Navajo economy steadily overhauled, passed, and then far surpassed the subsistence sector. Wages came to comprise 95 percent or more of total Navajo income, and absolute income levels rose rapidly. All of this economic resurgence put new life into many trading posts, which steadily transformed themselves from country general stores into rural supermarkets selling a wide range of processed foodstuffs.

The Navajo market became increasingly important to retailers and wholesalers in Southwestern cities and towns. Even radio stations began to cater to that market, hiring Navajo language announcers and "disc jockeys" to broadcast at certain hours, if not during the entire day. The structure of the Navajo language is such that "advertisements" came out virtually commands, to which Navajos unaccustomed to such propaganda responded with near unanimity. The favorite brand of condensed milk purchased throughout the reservation changed almost overnight, for example, when a milk company purchased advertising time.

One of the Navajo language broadcasters emerged as a principal candidate for Tribal Chairman in the hotly contested 1962 election. Jones ran for re-election against Samuel Billison and Raymond Nakai, the announcer. Nakai won the three-way race, and took office on April 13, 1963. He was able to win re-election in 1966.

Legislation designed to create the Great Society vision of President Lyndon Johnson drastically altered conditions among the Navajos during Nakai's second term. The Office of Economic Opportunity provided a major new conduit of federal funds for the Navajo people, with a charter enabling it to accomplish things the Bureau of Indian Affairs had never been able even to dream of trying. This new federal agency spawned numerous programs specially tailored to Navajo needs.

Both outstanding and controversial has been *Dinebeiina Nahiilna Be Agaditahe,* which might be translated as "Attorneys Contributing to Revitalizing 'The People's' Economic Liveli-

84

ERSMITHING was introduced by the Spanish-Americans in the 19th Century.
Navajo soon learned to make jewelry from United States and Mexican coins,
from these beginnings the Navajo have developed an art that has brought them
ld fame.

hood." In other words, DNA provides legal aid to poor Navajos with funds provided by the Office of Navajo Economic Opportunity (ONEO). Starting in April, 1967, DNA opened 19,600 cases within two years, and in time completed 15,418 of them. DNA initially tackled the Tribal Chairman, the Tribal Council, its general counsel and its own Navajo Legal Aid Service. The original non-Indian director aroused so much opposition that OEO made 1969 funding contingent upon his resigning. Leo Haven, a Navajo sociologist, replaced Ted Mitchell, but kept him working in the DNA program. By 1970, DNA's fourteen attorneys and ninety employees operated on an annual budget of over one million dollars. A third of its employees served as lay counselors representing clients in Navajo Tribal Court, where attorneys are forbidden. With offices in Chinle, Crownpoint, Shiprock and Tuba City as well as Window Rock, DNA exceeded in size the office of Arizona's Attorney General. Among other actions, DNA persuaded a federal court to overturn an Arizona welfare regulation requiring a parent to file paternity or non-support suits to qualify for Aid to Families with Dependent Children payments.

ONEO helped to finance day-care centers for working mothers at Fort Defiance and Shiprock, operated by Indian Aide, Inc., a non-profit organization. The Fort Defiance Center opened

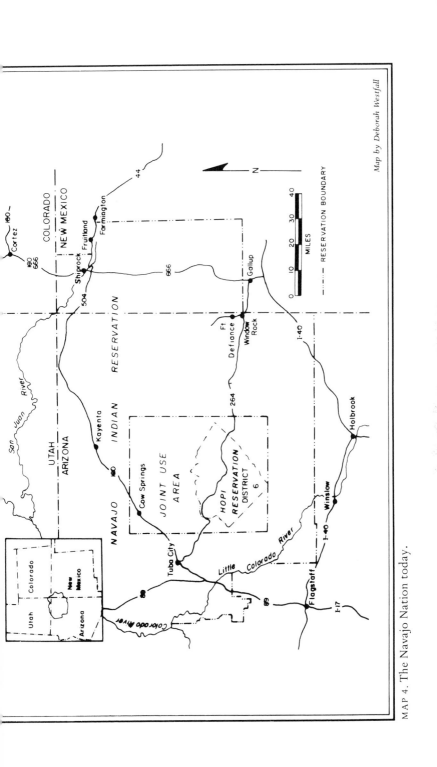

MAP 4. The Navajo Nation today.

Map by Deborah Westfall

in a building of Good Shepherd Mission, charging poverty level mothers one dollar weekly. Other ONEO programs improved Navajo homes, attacked alcoholism, provided community assistance and subsidized emigration. ONEO received over $5,500,000 in federal funds for its varied programs in the 1970 fiscal year.

So much impact did ONEO's multiple program achieve that the head of the Office of Navajo Economic Opportunity became a major and highly visible policy maker and source of patronage. He assumed a key role in tribal political affairs. Consequently, by the time the 1970 elections were held, Peter MacDonald, having resigned as head of ONEO to campaign for the Chairmanship, defeated Nakai and took office January 5, 1971, as leader of all the Navajo people. Wilson Skeet, another World War II Navajo code-talker, was elected vice-chairman. MacDonald won re-election as chairman in 1974.

As the elected chief executive of the largest native American group in the United States, MacDonald speaks with great authority in any gathering of Indian leaders. He wields significant political influence in Washington, and certainly on the Congressional delegations of the states of Arizona and New Mexico where most Navajos reside, plus Congressmen from districts in Utah and Colorado that include part of the Navajo Reservation or are adjacent to it. Symbolic of growing Navajo political power have been

89

federal appointments. Chairman MacDonald was named in November, 1971, to the National Public Advisory Committee on Regional Economic Development. This twenty-five-member panel advises the Secretary of Commerce. Navajo Community College President Ned A. Hatathli was named to the Western States Regional Manpower Advisory Committee, and an Indian Education Subcommittee of the National Council on Indian Opportunity.

More indicative of growing Navajo political power was the appointment of the first Navajo Director of the Window Rock Area Office of the Bureau of Indian Affairs in the spring of 1971. MacDonald set this as one of his goals for his first years in office. The Bureau transferred elsewhere the non-Indian Graham Holmes, Area Director since 1966. Then the Bureau transferred Navajo Anthony Lincoln from his desk as Associate Commissioner of Education and Programs in Washington to the Area Directorship. Son of former Navajo Chief Justice Murray Lincoln, the younger Lincoln thereby became the first Navajo Area Director in the Bureau of Indian Affairs.

Less than five years later, Chairman MacDonald demonstrated his power by forcing the Commissioner of Indian Affairs to transfer Lincoln. In January, 1976, Commissioner Morris Thompson offered the choice of accepting a new job as Southwest Field Coordinator in the Phoenix

Area Office or being fired.

MacDonald and other Navajo spokesmen loom larger and larger in state politics in New Mexico and Arizona. This is particularly true since those counties with majority Navajo population were included in the federal voter registration program along with counties in southern states with majority black populations.

In 1974, Chairman MacDonald spoke out in favor of Mexican-American Democratic party candidates for the governorships of Arizona and New Mexico. The Navajo voting allegiance to the Republican party generated during the 1930s was shattered, and both MacDonald-supported gubernatorial candidates won. Outraged Republicans in the national administration launched investigations of tribal fiscal management through the Federal Bureau of Investigation and the Phoenix U. S. Attorney's office. Early in 1976, U. S. Senator Barry Goldwater publicly called for the General Accounting Office to audit the tribe's accounts. Navajo Republicans commented that they could no longer be certain that Goldwater was a "friend of the Indian."

Troubles piled up for the Navajo Nation on other fronts.

Federal judges during the 1970s consistently decided against the Navajos in a suit filed in the previous decade by the Hopi tribal government. The Hopi leaders sought to oust Navajo families from part of the area the president had set aside for Hopis and other Indians in 1882. District Judge James A. Walsh imposed a fine of $250 daily beginning May 29, 1974, because Navajo officials had not obeyed a 1972 court order to reduce the number of Navajo-owned livestock grazing on the disputed land. After various appeals, Judge Walsh reaffirmed on April 7, 1977, that the Navajo Nation was liable for about $250,000 for not complying with his earlier order.

CONTINUING PROBLEMS

The emerging political strength of the Navajo tribal leadership and degree of industrialization achieved by no means solve all the problems of the rapidly expanding Navajo population. Sheer numbers in themselves pose fundamental difficulties to tribal government, the states where Navajos live, and to the nation. Navajo reservation population exceeded 150,000 persons by 1977, as improved health services have lowered the Navajo death rate and counterbalanced subsidized emigration to cities.

Dependence upon huge federal subsidies remained the weakest aspect of Navajo nationalism. Early in 1977, the General Accounting Office reported that $808 million in public funds went to the reservation during the three previous fiscal years. The GAO estimated annual federal support at $281.4 million in fiscal 1975, and then to $287.7 million in fiscal year 1976.

The latter figure was an average of $1,918 for each Navajo estimated to live on the reservation.

Tribal Budget. Despite its $13 million annual income from mineral royalties, the Navajo tribal government for several years has been spending beyond its current income — much of which should be considered capital payments rather than income. The 1971-72 budget exceeded $18 million, an increase of more than $2 million over the previous year. Major increases reflecting Chairman MacDonald's program included $1 million for a school clothing program, over half a million dollars for a Community Works Program, and over one-third of a million dollars for building local Chapter Houses. Area Director Lincoln has warned that tribal government must begin to balance its budgets.

Unemployment. In public speeches, Chairman MacDonald estimated the Navajo reservation unemployment rate at 65 percent and increasing. He calculated that 2,000 Navajos entered the labor market annually. While the basic extractive industries provided many jobs for Navajos, the tribe encountered difficulties diversifying industrial employment. In mid-1971, the Tribe sued one Arizona company for $1 million dollars it had loaned the company to establish a mobile home-trailer manufacturing plant on the reservation. The Navajos charged fraud. The nation-wide cut-back in space hardware acquisition in 1971 affected an electronics firm operating at Page since 1967. Having trained Navajos under the Bureau of Indian Affairs contract, and employed them, Vostron Industries announced in October, 1971, that it would close its Page plant within three months, ending thirty to forty jobs.

Investigators from the Department of Interior, the Federal Contract Compliance Office, and the Equal Employment Opportunity Commission early in January, 1972, began to look into Navajo complaints of job discrimination against major reservation corporate employers. Navajos charged the Salt River Project, Bechtel Corporation, and Morrison-Knudson Co., as well as the Laborers and Operating Engineers Unions with breaking agreements preferentially to hire Navajos.

The tribal government employed federal funds to create some additional employment on the reservation. The Bureau of Indian Affairs turned over to the Navajo Work Experience Program money that would otherwise be paid to jobless workers in assistance grants. The Bureau augmented this sum with a $30 monthly incentive fund. The Navajo Work Experience Program paid each worker the total amount, developing projects on which to employ the workers and supervising them. Its most popular projects involved home improvements and repairs.

Workers, averaging 500 monthly in fiscal year 1969, and 775 monthly in 1970, also repaired roads and fences and corrals, chopped and hauled wood for the elderly and disabled, improved water supplies and sanitation facilities, assisted in schools and hospitals, and produced handicraft products.

A massive job training program began on the reservation in 1973 under the Comprehensive Employment Training Act. By 1975, its budget reached $19 million. By late 1976, however, money ran out and some 1,000 Navajos had to be laid off. More than $9 million to hire perhaps 2,000 persons would not become available until early 1977.

Welfare. In spite of the massive efforts of the ONEO and tribal government, thousands of Navajos remained in real material need. Roughly 23,000 Navajos required welfare assistance from the Bureau of Indian Affairs at the end of 1970, apart from state welfare assistance efforts. Trying to improve the situation, the Navajo Tribe in mid-1971 assumed direction of the Federal food program for needy families. Signing an agreement with the Department of Agriculture, the tribal government brought into a single program distribution efforts previously fragmented under the states of Arizona, New Mexico and Utah. As the transfer was made, officials estimated that perhaps 83,000 Navajos would be eligible to receive food commodities. This implied that the tribe would be warehousing and distributing 3,000,000 pounds of food every month. Chairman MacDonald hailed the administrative change as an "historic occasion of Navajos taking control of their own program." The Department of Agriculture even attempted to cater to Navajo food preferences (as it perceived them) by supplying pinto beans, fortified flour, iron-enriched cereal and canned butter. These supplemented the standard twenty foods: dried and evaporated milk, cheese, canned fruits, vegetables, meats and poultry, lard, syrup, dried eggs, peanut butter, flour, corn meal, rice, macaroni, etc.

Alcoholism. The Navajos have not escaped many of the social problems that plague other ethnic groups suffering from chronic high unemployment and forced adjustment to the different cultural patterns of a dominant society. Symbolic of the tremendous alcoholism problems among Navajos was the first alcoholic treatment and recovery facility on an Indian reservation in the U. S. Twin Lakes Recovery Center opened in mid-1971, 17 miles north of Gallup, N. M., beside U. S. Highway 666. Designed to treat thirty patients at a time, the Center emphasized group therapy, vocational education, recreation, counseling and a balanced diet. The Office of Navajo Economic Opportunity financed Center construction and initial operation. The ONEO Executive Director at the time, Marshall Tome, estimated when this Center opened that there were over 2,000 Navajo chronic alcoholics.

The difficulties alcoholics encounter in earning a living and meeting the demands of national society carry over into urban environments in Denver, Los Angeles and other cities when such Navajos migrate seeking employment.

Employee Relations. For many years a small, intensely loyal cadre of tribal employees labored to keep tribal government going, and accomplishing vital tasks. With the tremendous growth of tribal bureaucracy, Navajo leaders found that they faced many of the same problems that other governments encounter. Friction between tribal leaders and bureaucrats surfaced in the fall of 1971 when the tribal police force walked out. The officers demanded overtime pay and uniform allowances. Tribal leaders exhorted the policemen to keep working pending Tribal Council action on their demands. Even after that crisis passed, the Navajo Nation at the end of 1976 still had to hire a non-Indian police superintendent. Worse, accusations of wrong-doing by tribal employees began to fly. Those accused ranged from a one-time clerk of the tribal court who pled guilty to embezzling $148, to the tribal chairman, who, in 1977, found it necessary to go through a jury trial in order to prove his innocence and thus protect his previously untarnished reputation.

97

CHRISTMAS, 1949, on the western Navajo Reservation. Many destitute Navajo famí
of well-planned, long range programs of economic betterment.

Courtesy of R. C. Euler

e receiving surplus government food such as potatoes and powdered milk in lieu

Housing. Many influences join to create an acute shortage of modern housing for those Navajos who work in tribal government, tribal enterprises, for the federal government or corporate employers on the reservation. The traditional hogans of the shepherds are located in the wrong places to house wage-workers in towns. They were built near springs and wells that provided stock water near good pastures. That meant that they were widely scattered, not constructed in compact settlements. As Navajos abandon the triadic hunting-food collecting-herding economy for wage labor, they must find new housing near their jobs. As they go to work, Navajos also acquire new wants for larger houses with furnishings such as stoves, clothes washers, dryers, easy chairs, beds and tables they have learned to use in school, see advertised on television and in non-Indian homes they visit.

The tribal government and several federal agencies have moved to construct modern housing for wage workers located where their jobs are. At the end of April, 1971, contracts were signed for the first Federal Housing Administration-approved project on an Arizona reservation. These provided for a $2.8 million dollar program to build 186 units at Fort Defiance. The only Indian licensed as a Class B contractor in Arizona — a Navajo, of course — worked with the prime contractor. The Bureau of Indian Affairs and Public Health Service joined in site preparation. The Minnesota Title Co. wrote title insurance and First Federal Savings and Loan Association (Phoenix) made a mortgage loan.

In late June, 1971, work started on the largest federally funded housing development yet undertaken on an Indian reservation, again for Navajos. Costing $4 million, this Shiprock, New Mexico, project is designed to place 214 single family dwellings and forty-one apartments on 180 acres. The Shiprock Nonprofit Housing and Community Development Corporation planned park and recreational facilities on the land, including the town's first swimming pool. A vice-president of Fairchild Camera and Instrument Corp., that employed 900 Navajos in its Shiprock semiconductor assembly plant, served as president of the housing authority.

Early in 1975, a Navajo member of the American Indian Movement and a score of his followers occupied the factory. This action diminished Navajo industrial employment.

At the beginning of 1971, planners began designing 700 new low-rent housing units for the Navajo Housing Authority to erect at thirty-five different locations on the reservation. The project sought to make available three to five bedroom homes renting from $55 per month up. The General Accounting Office estimated federal investment in reservation housing as $25 million during fiscal years 1974, 1975 and 1976.

Higher Education. The tremendous expansion of federal educational facilities for Navajo children after World War II greatly increased the number of elementary and secondary school graduates in the total Navajo population. As mineral royalties poured into tribal coffers, the Tribal Council appropriated scholarship funds to send Navajo secondary school graduates to college. Many ventured off to Northern Arizona University in Flagstaff, Arizona State University in Tempe, the University of Arizona at Tucson, the University of New Mexico at Albuquerque, Fort Lewis College in Durango, Colorado, and even more distant colleges and universities. Many obtained degrees in a wide variety of specialties and many are now enrolled in institutions of higher learning. Other Navajo students dropped out of school, however, and returned home or went to work at less skilled jobs than they might have obtained had they obtained college degrees. Moreover, many Navajo young people expressed the same feelings that have led cities all over the United States to set up local community colleges. They did not want to have to move so far away from home to attend college. Tempe and Tucson are in rather hot lowlands from the viewpoint of the Navajo plateau dweller living a mile or so high, and like the University of New Mexico, the universities there cope with large enrollments. Navajo students have protested that the Northern Arizona

University curriculum is not relevant to their needs.

The Office of Navajo Economic Opportunity consequently granted the Navajo Tribe funds with which to establish its own community college. Navajo Community College came into official being on July 1, 1968. It actually began teaching on January 20, 1969, sharing the buildings of the Bureau of Indian Affairs secondary school at Many Farms. The tribal government made available 1,200 acres at Tsaile Lake for a college campus, and plans for buildings for 1,500 students were finished by the end of 1970. Tribal and federal officials dedicated the permanent campus site on April 13, 1971, when over 500 students attended classes at the temporary site.

By mid-October of 1971, members of the Indian Affairs Subcommittee of the House Interior Committee were so eager to approve a bill appropriating federal funds to help with the estimated $16.5 million cost of building the new campus that they hardly paused to hear witnesses who traveled to the nation's capital to speak for the fledgling institution. Meanwhile, contracts had been let at the beginning of August for the first phase of construction costing almost $5 million. Some 600 students moved to the new campus in October, 1973. The school's third president, Thomas Atcitty, led a Navajo-style dedication on May 14, 1974. By then, the school could house 320 students in ten dormitories. Its buildings included a classroom facility, dining hall, gymnasium and student union.

Private agencies rallied to the cause of Navajo-controlled and oriented college education on this reservation. The Ford Foundation, for example, in 1971 granted $285,000 to expand the Community College's leadership training program. The Association of American University Presses donated 444 books to the College's Library in mid-1971. College President Ned A. Hatathli and his faculty members naturally welcomed such support from the private sector. They began to produce printed materials for the Navajo studies component of this tribal community college curriculum.

Like the faculty of Sinte Galeska College on the Rosebud Sioux Reservation (see THE SIOUX PEOPLE) the new college's instructors at Many Farms carried education out of the temporary classrooms to Navajo adults. They provided instruction at fifteen other settlements on the Reservation such as Nazlini, Rough Rock, Whippoorwill, Piñon, Lukachukai, Greasewood, Wheatfields, Rock Point and Cottonwood. By mid-1974, the college concentrated its off-campus instruction at a branch in Shiprock, New Mexico.

THE FUTURE

As the Navajos end the decade of the 1970's, certain predictions about their coming position

T HAND, a prominent Navajo, photographed at one of the important meetings.
Indians have many interesting and picturesque gatherings, some of which are of
rious nature while others are purely social. They always dress in their finest.

in the United States can be made with some assurance.

Population Trend. First of all, the Navajos are going to continue to be the largest single Indian polity in the U. S. in the foreseeable future. Already far larger than any other tribe, the Navajos continue to increase rapidly in numbers. There appears to be no reason to expect a quick decline in Navajo birth rates, and the very size and relative youth of the Navajo population means that it will increase considerably during the coming decade, at least. This burgeoning Navajo population is basic to many future expectations for Navajos, such as speculation that Navajo country may become the next state admitted to the Union, or at the very least, Navajo counties may be created in New Mexico and Arizona.

Indianness. Growing population size interacts with other influences such as increasing mineral royalty income, rising levels of formal education, and expanded and diversified work experience to augment the Navajo sense of Indianness and specifically of Navajoness. As Navajo tribal government leaders have become familiar with the power that they can wield in state and regional affairs, as Navajo population grows, and as Navajo personal and tribal income increases, Navajos more and more talk of a "Navajo nation."

Just what specific forms this growing ethnic consciousness will take during the years to come cannot very well be predicted at this writing. It will certainly, however, color Navajo relationships with public officials at all levels, with corporations doing business on the reservation or with tribal government off-reservation. It has already created a uniquely Navajo curriculum at Navajo Community College and in some secondary and elementary schools. This trend can be expected to continue. Navajo leaders imbued with the concept and goal of nationhood may aim toward political statehood, or Navajo control of existing counties in New Mexico and Arizona, including election of Navajos to state legislatures, as well as increasing Navajo administration of Federal programs.

Migration. The growing Navajo population within the reservation area of fixed agricultural and pastoral resources also makes fairly certain that Navajos will continue to move to metropolitan areas in search of employment and economic security. Navajo Community College could well prove to be a mixed blessing in this regard. It plans on a third of its projected enrollment pursuing academic studies with two-thirds of its students enrolled in vocational training oriented toward reservation job opportunities. Vocational training programs for poverty-stricken ethnic minorities elsewhere have ended up fitting

107

trainees only for migration, and the Navajo Community College may well find itself contributing to the migratory current.

Continuing Navajo migration means that Navajos as individuals will become increasingly familiar to residents of several major metropolitan centers in the Western states. These include Denver, Albuquerque, Phoenix, Los Angeles, the cities around San Francisco Bay and even Chicago. It means that more and more Navajos will compete with Blacks, Mexican-Americans and working class Anglo-Americans for inner-city employment, housing, education and even welfare benefits. Because of all the cultural adjustments a Navajo reservation-to-city migrant must make in order to succeed socially and economically, one must anticipate a relatively high rate of failure for some time into the future. The incidence of alcoholism that led tribal officials to found a treatment and recovery center near Gallup — a reservation-border town which itself will continue to be a major focus for Navajo drinking — will predictably carry over to the cities.

In much the same way, urban welfare agencies in cities where Navajos go in search of economic betterment must anticipate increased Navajo caseloads. Being human, Navajo migrants cannot be expected to perform any better as migrants learning to cope with over-grown metropolitan areas than any other ethnic group. Every such

108

group moving into U. S. major cities has at one time or another added to the welfare burden.

Factionalism. Political factions developed among the Navajo people decades ago. Major political factions have played some role in all recent elections of Tribal Chairmen and Councilmen. These factions are not going to disappear tomorrow. As a matter of fact, the growth of Navajo population can be expected to exert constantly increasing pressure toward even greater factionalism. The reservation-to-city migration current itself creates a newly important dimension to the factional split between reservation and off-reservation Navajo residents. Navajos inhabiting the "checkerboard area" in New Mexico east of the reservation proper have long constituted an identifiable political faction in tribal affairs. Living in an area where every other section of land is owned by non-Indians, those Navajos tend to regard themselves as step-children of reservation government. The land tenure structure fosters their permanent existence as a different interest-group from other Navajos. Urban Navajos in the off-reservation cities have not even every other land section to call their own. Thus, they are coming to constitute a new sort of faction that will grow in numbers in the future.

Because other native Americans all over the United States have moved to cities in great numbers, urban Navajos will be tempted to form political and social alliances with them. As such alliances emerge, they cannot help but influence tribal governance on the Navajo reservation.

Religion. Christian missionaries certainly will carry on their decades-old campaigns to convert Navajos to one or another denomination. They will continue to find that their culturally-biased Christian charity that often takes the form of giving "poor Navajos" used clothing and like good works actually alienates potential converts. Nonetheless, some Navajos will find personal salvation in Christian tenets, because of deep psychological needs. The same well-springs of personal dilemmas, frustrations and uncertainty that lead hundreds of Navajos to alcoholism as an escape motivate others to embrace Christianity, especially fundamentalist denominations, and its ethical system. Deeply religious Navajo Christians will not need alcohol to cope with problems.

Nor will members of the Native American Church. This will surely continue to be for some time the most important dissenting Christian influence among Navajos, numerically speaking. This denomination fuses elements of Christian belief with elements of native American belief. Its rituals center upon consumption by communicants of *peyote,* the top of a cactus plant known botanically as *Lophophora Williamsii.* A long series of court battles have more or less firmly established the freedom of worship of members of the Native American Church in various states under the Constitutional Bill of Rights. Yet this has not altered the Navajo tribal ban on peyotism. Many civil authorities continue to regard peyote as a narcotic. It is a hallucinogen.

Originally, a small number of Navajos took up peyotism from Ute Indians at Towaoc. As early as 1910, Navajos lived on Mancos Creek on the Ute Reservation; they provided the first converts. By the mid-1930's, five of these men had become the first Navajo peyote priests. They conducted meetings over a large region south of their homes. By 1940, they had made sufficient converts that a secondary peyote religious center arose in the Window Rock-Fort Defiance-Sawmill-Crystal-Tohatchi area. Local opposition led to the arrest of two of the pioneer peyote priests in 1938, when they served sixty-day sentences for possessing a narcotic on the reservation.

Not until 1940, however, did the Navajo Tribal Council outlaw the sale, use or possession of peyote. Tribal Chairman Jacob C. Morgan was a Christian missionary, trained at Hampton Institute. He also bitterly opposed Commissioner Collier, who made plain his official tolerance for the Native American Church. Vice-Chairman Howard Gorman was a Presbyterian strongly influenced by the medical missionary head of the Presbyterian hospital at

111

Ganado, outspoken Clarence Salsbury. Another leader of the anti-peyote movement, Councilman Roger Davis, also worked as a Christian missionary. Only one peyotist served on the Council and voted against the ordinance making peyote illegal and imposing a fine of $100 or/and imprisonment for nine months upon conviction in tribal court.

As a proponent of both native American religious freedom and autonomy of reservation governance, Commissioner Collier faced a dilemma when the Navajo Christian-dominated Council outlawed peyote. Recommending Federal approval of the ordinance, Collier also held that no Federal employee could enforce it. During the second World War, no Navajo policemen were paid from tribal funds. Lack of vigorous enforcement of the tribal anti-peyote legislation motivated some emotional opponents of the peyote movement to carry out private raids on peyote meetings to break them up. The Native American Church nonetheless continued to gain converts.

By 1954, the Navajo government paid a high proportion of policemen's salaries, and over a dozen persons were arrested on charges stemming from peyote use. Leaders of the peyote cult requested a hearing by the Tribal Council, which was held June 1-3, 1954. A pharmacological expert and an anthropologist retained by the Bureau of Indian Affairs in 1949 to study Navajo peyotism, testified. They listened to criticism from Council members who voiced an open desire to hear Salsbury. The tribe's General Counsel offered advice on legal points involved in the controversy.

The Navajo Tribal Council took no action. Thus, it allowed the 1940 ordinance to stand. There matters remained under the Paul Jones administration. When Raymond Nakai campaigned for the chairmanship, he stated that he favored religious freedom and knew nothing about peyotism. Members of the Native American Church interpreted this as favorable to their religious practices. These people constitute a significant portion of the Navajo electorate. The Navajo area coordinator for the Native American Church claimed membership cards for no less than 35,000 Navajo men, women and children by the middle of the 1960 decade.

The Native American Church and other peyotists have clearly demonstrated a dynamism of conversion among the Navajo people matched by no more traditional Christian denomination. There is every reason to anticipate, therefore, that Navajo membership in this church will continue to expand, and claims have already been advanced that a majority of the Navajo population already is affiliated with it.

Traditional Navajo religion concerned primarily with keeping people in harmony with nature through the supernatural so as to avoid

113

illness, certainly will not disappear in the immediate future. Twenty years of U. S. Public Health Service competition may have weakened demand for native cures, but clearly have not ended it. More serious long-range factors likely to weaken traditional religion are the Native American Church (Indian but not originally Navajo), formal Western-style education even in its Navajo Community College version with a significant Navajo cultural curriculum, and the stringent demands of learning complicated chants and myths in order to practice. Chairman Peter MacDonald, the first college graduate elected to head Navajo tribal government, himself dropped out of training to become a curer because of economic necessity after he spent almost a year studying. Later, when he could afford to study again, he chose to attend college and become a missile system engineer. Younger Navajos are likely to make the MacDonald-style choice oftener than they are to opt for the difficult apprenticeship of the would-be curer.

Continued Navajo reliance upon traditional curers and diagnosticians has encountered more resistance from the blue-collar peers of Navajo miners than from physicians. By later 1976, over eighty percent of the members of United Mine Workers Local 1620, District 22, were Navajos. A request that the union allow spending health care funds for tribal medicine men was turned

114

down by the union's top health program officials early in 1977.

On the other hand, the formal instructional techniques of Western Civilization had been brought to bear upon the task of training curers, possibly indicating a path to maintaining a corps of Navajo native practitioners. The National Institute of Mental Health underwrote a "medicine man training program" directed by John Dick at Rough Rock Demonstration School, which had at least one medicine man on its board. Interns received instruction in Blessing Way, Red Ant Way, Big Star Way, Male Arrow Shooting Way, Mountain Way and Against Evil Way.

Navajos will for some years at least continue to attend Pueblo Indian religious festivals, and to be influenced by them. Such influences are likely to diminish, however, as the Navajo population acquires more formal education. More important in the future is likely to be a pan-Indian religious movement being shaped by leaders from perhaps a dozen tribes in different parts of the United States. What seems unlikely to change is the fundamental religiosity of the Navajo people.

SUGGESTED READINGS

Books and scientific papers about Navajos are mountainous in quantity, partly because Navajos are nice people and cooperate with investigators. This listing emphasizes mainly discussions of topics we could hardly touch upon in our brief summary.

ABERLE, DAVID F. *The Peyote Religion Among the Navajo.* Chicago: Aldine Pub. Co., 1966.
Authoritative description and analysis of roots of major dissenting denomination.

ADAIR, JOHN, *Navajo and Pueblo Silversmiths.* Norman: University of Oklahoma Press, 1945.
Authoritative history and technical discussion, well illustrated.

AMSDEN, CHARLES AVERY, *Navaho Weaving.* Albuquerque: University of New Mexico Press, 1949.
Authoritative history and technical account, well illustrated.

DYK, WALTER, *A Navaho Autobiography.* New York: Johnson Reprint Corp. (1964) of Viking Fund Publication No. 8, 1947.
Anthropologist's transcription of an autobiography representative of the people and times of shepherding.

GILPIN, LAURA, *The Enduring Navajo.* Austin: University of Texas Press, 1968.

Coffee-table photographic record of some of The People from the Great Depression until the late 1960's by an eminent photographer.

HANNUM, ALBERTA, *Spin a Silver Dollar*. New York: Viking Press, 1944.
Very readable human-interest account of a trading post.

Paint the Wind. New York: Viking Press, 1958. Story of a young Navajo artist begun in the earlier volume, told in the same style.

KLAH, HASTEEN, recorded by Mary C. Wheelwright, *Navajo Creation Myth*. Santa Fé: Museum of Navajo Ceremonial Art, 1942. One ceremonialist's version of the emergence story.

KLUCKHOHN, CLYDE, *Navaho Witchcraft*. Boston: Beacon Press reprint, 1944.
Authoritative study of a subject seldom analyzed; important in general social science theory.

KLUCKHOHN, CLYDE, W. W. HILL AND L. W. KLUCKHOLN, *Navaho Material Culture.* Cambridge: Belknap Press of Harvard University Press, 1971.
Massive reference work by outstanding authorities.

KLUCKHOHN, CLYDE AND DOROTHEA C. LEIGHTON, *The Navajo*. Cambridge: Harvard University Press, 1946.

117

Excellent summary resulting from Indian Personality Study at time of World War II.

LEIGHTON, ALEXANDER H. AND DOROTHEA C. LEIGHTON, *The Navajo Door.* Cambridge: Harvard University Press, 1944 (New York: Russell & Russell, 1967).

Best introduction to cultural factors in well-being, though somewhat outdated.

LEIGHTON, DOROTHEA C. AND CLYDE KLUCKHOLN, *The Children of the People.* Cambridge: Harvard University Press, 1947.

Campanion volume to *The Navajo,* and a basic study.

LINK, MARTIN A. (ed.) *Navajo, A Century of Progress, 1868-1968.* Window Rock: The Navajo Tribe, 1968.

Tribal Government view of 100 years under the U. S. Well illustrated and interestingly written.

McCOMBE, LEONARD, EVON Z. VOGT AND CLYDE KLUCKHOLN, *Navaho Means People.* Cambridge: Harvard University Press, 1951.

Scientific and humane photographic study; the best extant view of Gallup in the Navajo world.

Navajo History. Many Farms: Navajo Community College Press, 1971.

Navajo pre-history as refined by tribal authorities and edited by Ethelou Yazzie.

NEWCOMB, FRANC J., *Hosteen Klah: Navaho Medicine Man and Sand Painter*. Norman: University of Oklahoma Press, 1964.

Biography of a ceremonialist who recorded creation story.

REICHARD, GLADYS A., *Spider Woman*. New York: Macmillan, 1934 (Glorieta: Rio Grande Press, 1968).

Anthropologist's fine account of family life, weaving and ceremonialism.

Dezba. New York: J. J. Augustin, 1939.

Anthropologist's fictionalized description of matron and family relationships.

Navajo Religion: A Study of Symbolism. New York: Bollingen Foundation, 1950 (New York: Pantheon Books, 1963).

Great synthesis by the foremost student. Numerous monographs describe and analyze specific ceremonials.

ROESSEL, ROBERT A., JR. AND OTHERS *Indian Communities in Action*. Tempe: Arizona State University, 1967.

One-time head of the experimental Rough Rock School advocates in this volume his educational philosophy.

SASAKI, TOM T., *Fruitland, New Mexico.* Ithaca: Cornell University Press, 1960.

Sobering policy-science analysis of federally financed resettlement program and Navajo social change.

SHEPARDSON, MARY AND BLODWEN HAMMOND, *The Navajo Mountain Community.* Berkeley: University of California Press, 1970.

Fairly technical anthropological analysis of what is often taken to be the most isolated and traditional Navajo population.

UNDERHILL, RUTH M., *Here Come the Navajo!* Lawrence: Haskell Institute, 1953.

Well-written and illustrated historical summary.

The Navajos. Norman: University of Oklahoma Press, 1956.

Equally well-written synthesis of Navajo society during historic times, readily available.

WYMAN, LELAND C., *The Red Antway of the Navaho.* Santa Fé: Museum of Navajo Ceremonial Art, 1965.

Account of ceremonial employed for kidney and bladder troubles attributed to urinating on an ant-hill.

Blessingway. Tucson: University of Arizona Press, 1970.

Three myth versions recorded by Berard Haile, O.F.M.

Beautyway, A Navaho Ceremonial. New York: Pantheon, Books, 1957.

Texts recorded by Berard Haile and Maud Oakes.

YOUNG, ROBERT W. *The Role of the Navajo in the Southwestern Drama.* Gallup: Gallup Independent, 1968.

Historical summary by foremost student and servant of the Navajos, emphasizing men whose contributions should be remembered.

YOUNG, ROBERT W. AND WILLIAM MORGAN, *Navajo Historical Selections.* Phoenix: Phoenix Indian School Printshop, 1954.

Selections from Navajo newspaper, in English and Navajo.

The four Indian Tribal Series publications referred to in the text are:

CASH, JOSEPH H., *The Sioux People (Rosebud),* 1971

EULER, ROBERT C., *The Paiute People,* 1972

EULER, ROBERT C. AND HENRY F. DOBYNS, *The Hopi People,* 1971

DOBYNS, HENRY F., *The Apache People (Coyotero),* 1971.

INDIAN TRIBAL SERIES
PUBLICATIONS

THE HAVASUPAI PEOPLE
    Dr. Henry F. Dobyns and Dr. Robert C. Euler
THE HOPI PEOPLE
    Dr. Robert C. Euler and Dr. Henry F. Dobyns
THE APACHE PEOPLE (COYOTERO)
    Dr. Henry F. Dobyns
THE SIOUX PEOPLE (ROSEBUD)
    Dr. Joseph H. Cash
THE PAIUTE PEOPLE
    Dr. Robert C. Euler
THE NAVAJO PEOPLE
    Dr. Henry F. Dobyns and Dr. Robert C. Euler
THE CROW PEOPLE
    Dale K. McGinnis and Dr. Floyd Sharrock
THE OSAGE PEOPLE
    Dr. W. David Baird
THE PAPAGO PEOPLE
    Dr. Henry F. Dobyns
THE YAKIMA PEOPLE
    Dr. Richard Daugherty
THE CHOCTAW PEOPLE
    Dr. W. David Baird
THE MESCALERO APACHE PEOPLE
    Dr. Henry F. Dobyns
THE CREEK PEOPLE
    Dr. Donald Green
THE SEMINOLE PEOPLE
    Dr. Charles H. Fairbanks
THE KALISPEL PEOPLE
    Dr. Robert Carriker
THE CHEROKEE PEOPLE
    Earl Boyd Pierce and Rennard Strickland
THE CHICKASAW PEOPLE
    Dr. W. David Baird
THE THREE AFFILIATED TRIBES
    Dr. Joseph H. Cash and Dr. Gerald Wolff
THE ONEIDA PEOPLE
    Dr. Cara Richards

THE COCOPAH PEOPLE
    Mrs. Anita Alvarez de Williams
THE COMANCHE PEOPLE
    Dr. Joseph H. Cash and Dr. Gerald Wolff
THE SOUTHERN UTE PEOPLE
    Dr. Robert Delaney
THE KENAITZE PEOPLE
    Dr. Robert E. Ackerman
THE CHITIMACHA PEOPLE
    Dr. Herbert T. Hoover
THE QUAPAW PEOPLE
    Dr. W. David Baird
THE NARRAGANSETT PEOPLE
    Dr. Ethel Boissevain
THE PONCA PEOPLE
    Dr. Joseph H. Cash and Dr. Gerald Wolff
THE KAW PEOPLE
    Dr. William E. Unrau
THE KICKAPOO PEOPLE
    Dr. George R. Nielsen
THE CHIPPEWA TRIBE (MINN.)
    Dr. Timothy Rouffs
THE SENECA PEOPLE
    Dr. George H. J. Abrams
THE WALAPAI PEOPLE
    Dr. Henry F. Dobyns and Dr. Robert C. Euler
THE OTOE-MISSOURIA PEOPLE
    Dr. R. David Edmunds
THE OTTAWA PEOPLE
    Dr. Joseph H. Cash and Dr. Gerald W. Wolff
THE COUSHATTA PEOPLE
    Dr. Bobby H. Johnson
THE PAWNEE PEOPLE
    Dr. Carl N. Tyson
THE MODOC PEOPLE
    Dr. Odie B. Faulk
THE WICHITA PEOPLE
    Dr. William W. Newcomb
THE POTAWATOMI PEOPLE
    Dr. Joseph H. Cash
THE ESKIMO PEOPLE
    Dr. Robert E. Ackerman

HENRY F. DOBYNS briefly studied various Navajo settlements between 1949 and 1959. He has taught anthropology at Cornell University, the University of Kentucky, Prescott College, and the University of Wisconsin – Parkside. He is author of *Spanish Colonial Tucson* (University of Arizona Press), and *Native American Historical Demography* (Indiana University Press) and numerous other books.

ROBERT C. EULER is anthropologist at Grand Canyon National Park. He led several student groups studying the impact of large-scale coal mining on Navajo families on Black Mesa in the late 1960s and early 1970s. Earlier he lived with a Navajo family for almost two years along the Little Colorado River while he carried on a study of their economic life. He has taught anthropology at Northern Arizona University, the University of Utah, Prescott College and Fort Lewis College.

124